A Letter to the American People

A LETTER TO THE

AMERICAN PEOPLE

BY LAWRENCE HUNT

G. P. PUTNAM'S SONS, NEW YORK

Designed by Robert Josephy

PRINTED IN THE UNITED STATES OF AMERICA

To My Wife

CONTENTS

A Letter to the American People

My Fellow Countrymen:

I shall use plain, blunt words to say plain, blunt things.

Many of you will never get this letter. Some of you will not like it. None of you will agree with all I say. But I hope that those of you who do read these words will think about them a bit.

We hear and read every day the pompous words of politicians, the glib words of pseudo intellectuals, and the smart words of newspaper columnists about this war and our part in it. You and I don't talk as they do, and in our hearts we don't believe the things some of them tell us. Now it is up to us to talk—to make our wishes known—and to act as a sufficient number of Americans (not all, by a long shot) have always acted when conscious of their duty and their danger. I think that there are still "a sufficient number" of us to do the job that must be done.

This letter, as letters go, is rather long, and so for convenience' sake I shall jot down a few headings.

OUR PONTIUS PILATES

Pontius Pilate still lives. Even now he exercises greater influence on our national thinking about foreign affairs than any other person living or dead. He strides the length and breadth of America, dinning his immortal philosophy of neutrality into our minds and hearts. You can hear him on the platform, over the radio, in the pulpit, at women's club meetings and labor union rallies. You can read his words in current books, in magazines and newspapers. A year ago he was saying "Wash your hands of this mess. I did once, and saved myself a lot of work and worry. That was none of my business. This is none of yours. So wash your hands of it now."

Today his words have changed, but his tune remains the same. "You may have forgotten it," he says, "but I adopted the 'short of war' policy when I was Governor. I put in a good word for Him, don't forget. Did all I felt was perfectly safe to do."

For the last twenty years we Americans have been fooling ourselves, as Pilate tried to do in another practical situation, when we've talked about America's foreign policy. We still are. It's not surprising. We have been deluged with a constant stream of propaganda about the "Crime of Versailles," "We won the war and what did we get?", "British imperialism," the pathetic spectacle of a gullible America caught in the wily intrigues of Old World diplomacy, "pulling England's chestnuts out of the fire," the "Merchants of Death," and the "Wall Street Bankers."

Today there's a new but equally polluted stream of propaganda luridly warning us against propaganda. The upshot of it all is that the thinking of many honest people has become confused, their nerves jangled, and their emotions jaded. And as a nation we have managed so far to escape from reality and the tough responsibilities of being a first-rate power. I don't mean that we have lost the puritanical vice of preaching to others, but we have failed to exercise the puritanical virtue of doing our share—and more, if need be—of the hard work our very greatness requires of us.

Who are these Pontius Pilate propagandists— these persons who are trying to take from us our moral manhood so that we shall feel a cold indifference toward right and wrong and who are giving consciously or unconsciously daily aid and comfort to Comrades Hitler and Stalin? Let's note a few of them briefly—very briefly—but mark them well. Then we'll go on to examine the slogans and catch phrases, the half truths and lies with which they try to confuse our minds and deaden our hearts.

Well—of course there are the political pimps soliciting the "foreign" vote. Like Hitler they assume that America is not a real nation with traditions, character, and courage but a glorified, polyglot boardinghouse in which discordant racial groups live restlessly side by side.

There are also the Gerald Nyes and the Burt Wheelers and the Hamilton Fishes who, just as Pilate was "willing to content the people" in his day (drugged as they were by the scribes and pharisees), are eager to please those people today who have been deluded and misinformed by their enemies inside as well as outside America. That type of politician is part of the steep price we pay for the democracy we cherish. Our faith in democracy is so genuine and so deep that we permit these Catilines to abuse our patience and even to advocate policies which would destroy that faith. But the demagogic politician is the least of our worries—he has an abnormal instinct for self-preservation and when he can no longer fool the people he will quickly follow them. I hardly need mention to you the Hugh Johnsons and Father Coughlins who have told you again and again that Britain and her allies on the one hand and Germany and her allies on the other are "all alike."

6

They resemble those unfortunate women who will do anything to hold attention. They grow worse with age. We can dismiss Mr. Charles Lindbergh as a remarkably able air pilot who with some effort, obvious sincerity, and much encouragement in certain quarters has achieved unquestioned rank as a leading American Nazi and richly deserves another medal from Hitler for pure devotion and hard work in his cause.

Hitler's most effective though unwitting allies in this country are among the so-called "intellectuals"—the propagandist historians, pseudo economists, and irresponsible journalists. Harry Elmer Barnes seems to be a pathological case whose pro-German and anti-British obsessions have apparently become too extreme for the Scripps-Howard press to feature. The glib Stuart Chase, the shallow John T. Flynn, the whining Oswald Villard remind us of those writers, familiar to every generation, whose words are "full of sound and fury, signifying nothing."

These men hardly deserve mention—even in a letter. One or two of them will achieve a minor footnote in some Ph.D. thesis of the future. But it is well to keep them in our mental files now that we must struggle to survive as a free and God-fearing people in our English-speaking civilization.

There was a time when outstanding men went

into the academic profession—with all the moral, mental, and physical attributes and appurtenances of manhood. Some still do. In the ranks of scholars and teachers are several of our greatest citizens. Men like James B. Conant and Samuel Eliot Morison of Harvard, Charles Seymour of Yale, Walter P. Hall of Princeton, Allan Nevins and James T. Shotwell of Columbia, Theodore Clarke Smith of Williams, Frank P. Graham of North Carolina, Harry Woodburn Chase of New York University —you know them and many, many more. And yet, these gentlemen adorn the most undisciplined and ethically irresponsible of all the professions—a profession which has become increasingly the habitat and refuge of a neutral sex, far removed from the earthy passions, the normal emotions, the spiritual values and moral driving force of ordinary men and women. The great majority of the academic profession are just as scrupulous and honorable as the great majority in the other professions, but the distinguishing trait in their relationships toward their shysters and humbugs is a peculiar timidity and a refusal to deal with them as rigorously as lawyers and doctors do with their erring brethren. They courageously admit this in private.

"Academic freedom" is as vital to the body politic as lungs to the human body. All the more need and care therefore that it should be kept healthy and clean by those who enjoy it and that it should not become a glittering slogan to protect the incompetent and the mentally dishonest. The academic shyster should be outlawed by his colleagues as quickly and as ruthlessly as the corrupt judge is removed from the bench or the unscrupulous lawyer is disbarred. The government must not do it—far better to suffer the present evils. Hitlerism is no cure for the ills of democracy. But the academic profession alone can and should do its own housecleaning.

You have probably noticed with mingled amusement and disgust those intellectuals who are sophomoric in their sensitivity to criticism from the outside world. They loudly, bitterly and often properly denounce statesmen, judges, big businessmen. But if some of their own group are in turn similarly attacked they yell bloody murder and wave the flag of academic freedom. In other words, they simply can't "take it." In their own peculiar way they are just as intolerant as the shortsighted type of businessman who is a liberal while sipping his liqueur but not when dealing with his employees. The business-hating intellectual and the red-baiting businessman are fundamentally Tweedledum and Tweedledee.

I think this sensitivity of certain intellectuals is partly caused by another sophomoric mental state —a belief that they are mentally superior to those of us, for example, who earn our living as businessmen or lawyers. They are obviously more articulate, they know more words, and quite probably they got "better marks" in school or college than those engaged in more vulgar pursuits. And they cling, at times rather frantically, to their adolescent belief in themselves and a comforting scorn toward the rest of us. It's a strange priesthood they've created and its creed seems to be criticism with impunity toward all, immunity from criticism by any.

Most members of the academic profession don't really believe in such a priesthood but, like their fellow citizens in business and in some labor unions, they have been too slow and too timid in dealing with the unscrupulous element in their ranks. I think, moreover, that our academic friends will probably admit, in private, that the greatest weakness of their great profession is that its members are rarely compelled to make decisions which have definite and almost immediate consequences. The businessman and lawyer must make those decisions constantly in order to carry on. Naturally many wrong decisions are made, but partly as a result of making them a reasonable degree of tolerance is shown toward those who make them and suspicion and contempt are felt for the intellectual perfectionist who does not make decisions but bewails the wrong ones. The man who deals in decisions rather than in criticism tries to see the "end figure." That sometimes requires both mental and moral courage. Too many of our intellectuals lack the gumption to grasp a whole situation; they nervously and confusedly deal with a small part.

Their attitude toward the present war and America's relation to it is a tragic example of their great weakness. Like all decent, freedom-loving people, our college presidents and professors loathed Nazism. They were acutely aware of some of its vilest aspects. But, when the time finally came, with the outbreak of the war, for a hard decision by their own country, they were either mute or tried to find an escape in nervously talking about certain aspects of the situation. Some of them may have been fooled or bulldozed by the propaganda of certain other intellectuals. Whatever the reason, the so-called "leaders of American thought" failed as leaders. After the Germans invaded Holland and Belgium, a few important academic persons falteringly spoke the faith that was in them—along with and behind many less articulate people. Archibald MacLeish with winning sincerity and melancholy charm admitted in effect that he and his fellow intellectuals had been damn fools in playing the cynic rather than the man during the last twenty years.

But, I repeat, our academic and intellectual leaders fell down. That happened in another country. A truly great intellectual, a German named Thomas Mann, told the tragic truth when in 1937 he wrote his immortal letter to the dean of the philosophical faculty of the University of Bonn: "The German universities share a heavy responsibility for all the present distresses which they called down upon their heads when they tragically misunderstood their historic hour and allowed their soil to nourish the ruthless forces which have devastated Germany morally, politically, and economically."

Because our academic friends are not constantly required to make decisions—because life does not jerk them up every day—they are in danger of forgetting that they belong to the most influential of the professions and that they can exercise more power over the ultimate destinies of men than those of us engaged in the so-called "active life." Their sense of responsibility should be in proper proportion to their influence and power. When they are irresponsible, the damage done is very great and persists for a long time. The reason is, of course, that they are dealing with the minds and spirits of men. For example, if a historian makes in a book a false or unfair statement of historic facts, not only his students but also the newspaper editor and the columnist and the radio commentator, too rushed by their daily work to verify or correct the statement, are likely to pick

12

it up and pass it along to the "man in the street," whose opinions and decisions are accordingly influenced. Such irresponsibility imperils the influence of the honest intellectual and, in these times, is a menace to the public.

Yes—I'm thinking of several people in the so-called academic world—of those intellectuals, indifferent to moral values, who have misled many honest, well-meaning citizens with their propaganda against the democracies and who today still whimper and whine for a peace without honor and without freedom. Harry Elmer Barnes is an example. Somewhat typical is a Dartmouth professor named Stilwell, who, a few days after Hitler's Huns had invaded Holland and Belgium and slaughtered thirty thousand citizens of Rotterdam "as a lesson," was reported in the New York press as having told a crowd of susceptible adolescents that Hitler had "sharp Yankee insight" and that Hitler's peace would be no worse than the Versailles treaty because "it couldn't be."

I mean, among others, Charles A. Beard. No one, to my knowledge, has questioned his patriotism. He has many devoted admirers, especially among the younger intellectuals. I have no doubt that he personally disapproves of the Nazis, their tortures of free-thinking people, their concentration camps, and their objectives. (The same was true of some professors in the German universities

13

mentioned by Thomas Mann.) As you know, he has a big reputation as a historian, and the public naturally expects him, as a historian, to present the facts of history with scrupulous care.

In his recent book *A Foreign Policy for America,* Mr. Beard is guilty of grave irresponsibility. In that book he is no longer the respectable historian but an unscrupulous propagandist. Twisting of facts, nondisclosure of vital evidence, downright "misstatements" are used with all the skill of the Nazi propagandists—and doubtless to their satisfaction—to keep us neutral.

His book is a plea for an isolationist foreign policy based on what he alleges to be American history. Beard purports to argue against "entanglements in the age-long coalitions of Europe and Asia" of which, he assumes, the present war is just another example. He evidently thinks isolationism will smell sweeter if called by a different name—"continentalism." He asserts that the main tradition of our government has been a strict and exclusive concentration on domestic problems and tries to prove it very largely by ignoring or distorting or abusing the foreign policies of our greatest Secretaries of State, including Henry Clay, Daniel Webster, John Hay, Elihu Root, and Cordell Hull, of Thomas Jefferson in the case of the Monroe Doctrine, and of Presidents McKinley, Theodore Roosevelt, Taft, Wilson, and Franklin

D. Roosevelt. And he concludes his book by urging us to be nice and polite toward all nations, good or bad, and to refrain from making any comments on the "manners and morals of other countries," including, of course, Hitler's Germany.

Like a Nazi propagandist, Beard realizes the necessity and seems to relish the task of "smearing" the great statesmen and historians of the past whose influence he wishes to destroy. As many of you know, Admiral Mahan of the United States Navy was the author of one of the most distinguished books in modern times—*The Influence of Sea Power upon History*. Beard bravely hurls insults at the great man's ghost—"veritable ignoramus," "propagandist," "distorter of history," "full-blown imperialist," his book "found a hearty response in power-hungry minds" such as Theodore Roosevelt. (Have you never noticed how intellectuals like Beard condemn "name calling" by their opponents?)

A few of you may have read the cool analysis of Beard's book by the judicious Professor Allan Nevins which appeared in the New York *Times* on May 26, 1940. Professor Nevins points out that Beard has won his place among historians "by applying a smart, hard materialism to the interpretation of history, and thus often arriving at a clever simulacrum of Truth rather than Truth itself." Professor Nevins says that "two characteristics of the book are especially notable. The first is this frigid indifference to moral considerations. . . . The other remarkable characteristic of the book is the way in which it wrests history to support special pleading."

As a clever propagandist, Beard knows how to quote a part of a historic statement out of its context so as to create a false impression on the reader's mind. Thus he quotes a few words from a famous letter from Jefferson to Monroe so that the uninformed reader would be led to believe that Jefferson was an isolationist. He does not quote the chief part of the letter, in which Jefferson urged that the United States unite its forces with Britain's to protect this hemisphere against continental Europe which was then in the iron grip of autocracy. (I'll mention that later on.) Allan Nevins also referred caustically to several "misstatements" by Beard. But Beard's unscrupulous propaganda will probably deceive many citizens who have never read Mr. Nevins's forthright exposure of it. That is why irresponsible intellectuals who purport to be honest scholars do terrific harm and, in these days, are a public menace. There is no need for me to say more about Beard at this point. But mark him well. He is (unconsciously, no doubt) Hitler's cleverest academic ally in America.

The smart pseudo intellectuals spend so much

time and effort at playing God that they forget or cannot grasp the simple forthright values by which most of us plain people live. They set themselves up and try to sell us their wares as being "realistic" or "objective" or "impartial." You and I know, if we take the trouble to look closely at these humbugs, that they nervously "go to pieces" when met with a hard but simple truth and a tough but obvious fact. They squirm and squeal their way into an unreal blueprint world in which there are no embarrassing standards of good and evil, no stern decisions to be made, no choice to be taken, for instance, between the King James Bible and *Mein Kampf,* no heartfelt sacrifices and no sweating toil, and where they can comfortably and cleverly talk and talk until doom's day while we listen, applaud, and pay them. Every age has had such jabberers, those nervous and naïve persons who chatter feverishly on the sidelines of human life. In ordinary times we can afford to put up with them and toss them pennies if for no other reason than that some amuse us with their antics. But these are not amusing times. Work must be done, tears must flow, and blood must be shed before we can again laugh as free men in a free world. And so I ask you not to waste your precious moments now on these mentally gaudy, morally impotent people and, above all, do not let them fool you with self-deceiving words which must

17

make the Nazi-Communist propagandists gasp with envy.

Some well-meaning preachers give their support, quite unconsciously, to the theory of propagandists like Beard that Uncle Sam is all stomach and no soul. They valiantly thunder that it's a sin to steal a pin, but they sanctimoniously squeak to us brothers and sisters about "peace" while the Nazis try to reduce our civilization to a shambles and the surviving men, women, and children into slaves. To be fair, our clergy has made, by and large, since the outbreak of the war a much manlier showing than the academic crowd, most of whom have been, until lately, strangely mute as so-called "leaders of American thought." And yet, the pulpits have their share—too big a share—of men utterly incapable of righteous anger and of wielding, in God's name, the sword of Gideon. When next you go to church, I suggest that you be attentive enough to examine the leader of your flock. Is he a real man to lead you to do good even though it hurts or just a tame mouse to make you feel good, whatever the future cost? Is he in the mighty tradition of Saint Augustine, John Knox, Henry Ward Beecher, and the late Cardinal Mundelein? Or does he chant with "Father" Divine "Peace—it's wonderful?" My guess is that God is tired of hearing Pontius Pilate in so many pulpits.

I may not find the time in this letter to discuss the sanctimonious slogans of certain pacifist and isolationist preachers. They don't do nearly as much harm as our intellectual milksops who disguise themselves in so-called "scholarship." This is partly because many of us have become good-naturedly accustomed to mealy-mouthed sermons. But be on your guard against the hazy messenger of the Word. And remember that the Lord likes a *man* in His house the same as anywhere else.

Behind the lines of the well-known propagandists, such as Beard, often of equal professional rank, are some pathetic and hard-toiling people—the academic munition workers who supply them with firecrackers to dazzle and deafen the public. You know them. They earnestly strive, by putting one footnote after another, to win a feeble academic fame while their glib colleagues reap the profits. Like their more opulent faculty associates, they are immersed in the obscure and are victims of hysteria or amnesia (depending on their temperaments) when confronted by the crude, tough facts of this world such as *Mein Kampf*, the Nazi-Soviet alliance, the machine-gun slaughter of civilians, and the torture of the concentration camps. We must not be too harsh with them or make them scapegoats for their academic brothers. Nor should we begrudge them too much their anemic ecstasies when they discover for their blatant colleagues a glittering but irrelevant bit of historical gossip. They "must live somehow."

However, they deserve at least casual attention from us and from truly learned and honest-minded scholars because it is vital that our thinking be not bombed and deranged by the obscure, the trivial, and the insincere data of so-called "research men" and their mouthpieces. Even those who are sincere often miss the whole spirit of an age in the frantic search for a footnote. And those who are not honest are simply working the Nazi technique of propaganda. I mention these isolationist "scholars" because we must clear a lot of smelly rubbish out of our minds and force ourselves again and again and again to face manfully the great, sometimes harsh and sometimes beautiful facts of the world in which we and our children live. We must not duck down blind alleys to escape the main, straight, and often hard road to national and personal freedom and self-respect.

I'm sure most of you will understand when I use words like "freedom" and "self-respect." For nearly twenty years they were scornfully discarded by our pseudo intellectuals and are shunned or soiled today by those propagandists who evidently think of America as a luxurious pigsty completely shut off from the outside world. You remember the "disillusioned" novelists and poets after the last war who clothed their mental and moral impotence in the language of the brothel and titillated the adolescent and the jaded with their findings from the garbage cans and slop jars of human life. Well, that nasty and sordid materialism which denies the philosophy of Plato and the life of Christ—and our everyday experience for that matter—that materialism is one of the most subtle appeals of the isolationist and pro-Nazi propagandists. Please bear that constantly in mind when we come, as we soon shall, to the slogans and falsehoods of the hog-pen isolationists. We can understand the allure of a dazzling and selfish "materialism," and in tranquil times many of us can temporarily afford and most of us certainly do succumb to it. But not now. We must act like men and "put away childish things."

It's too bad that we are compelled to speak so plainly about our "intellectuals" and especially our academic friends, most of whom are really decent, hard-working fellows; but they have become too self-sanctified, too removed from the healthy moralities of life and the basic ethics of thought, too oblivious of the standards in which we plain people believe. Many of them carelessly and selfishly forget that their words are often given weight because their audience is mindful of the institutions they represent—institutions of learning, of great prestige, with many warm loyalties and with noble traditions of public service. Yes—they should

21

have a drubbing—an awakening—a moral and intellectual strengthening of their training and outlook and a vigorous cleansing of their ranks. The best of them know it. All they need—and it's a good deal—is the courage to do it.

Now then, before we "get down to cases" with the unscrupulous propaganda of the Beard type of isolationist, I want to warn you against one other general type of person who spreads, quite unconsciously as a rule but all the more successfully, the things Hitler wants us to think. I mean the man whom John Bunyan named "Mr. Facing-both-ways"—the sleek "good fellow" who "can't be bothered" and lazily appeals to an utterly perverted sense of justice with the phrase "on the other hand." In the normal course of life you and I use that phrase as a brake on hasty judgments, as a sort of formula to be fair in our opinions of our neighbor's deeds, as a balance in a warm argument. But, mind you, always in reference to the differences which exist within a civilized group. (If you think the Nazis are civilized, then don't read this letter.)

Yes, in everyday life we should say, again and again, "on the other hand." It's so easy to harm people and so hard to help them. *But*—if we're decent (a word that our smart pseudo intellectuals scorn and fear), we don't speak that way about the murderer or kidnaper or traitor. We say "shoot 'em." That is what we must say about the nastiest lawbreakers of all—the Nazis. And yet, it's so easy for some of us to use any refuge—any escape from the truth. Easy at the time. Not later—the French men and women who were betrayed by their Other Handers could tell you about that, if they were free. Can we Americans still face a grim, hard truth—with fight and laughter and "Rebel yells" and "Battle Hymns"? Or shall we dumbly and blindly slog along after the Beards and Coughlins, Mr. Facing-both-ways and the Other Handers, down the road of national and personal ruin? I'm sure we won't. There are enough of us —a "sufficient number" of us who just won't do it. We'll fight.

SOME POPULAR NARCOTICS

One of the favorite sports of professors and writers who have consciously or unconsciously misled and misinformed the American public in recent years has been to deride the motives which caused and the purposes which inspired America's entry into the last World War. They have created bogies and scarecrows, naming them the "Wall Street Bankers" and the "Merchants of Death" and depicting them as beguiling and forcing the American people against their will to take part in the war.

That just isn't so, and you and I know it.

These and other slogans and falsehoods spread at first by our own professors and writers and later repeated incessantly by Hitler are simply popular narcotics with which we have deadened the pangs of conscience caused by our great betrayal of the best hopes of mankind when we quit the peace. Yes—narcotics to banish the hot twinges of shame when we stop to think how loudly we have talked and how little we have done to make law and reason supreme in the affairs of men. Today they help some people to forget the menace of Hitler, the demands of ordinary human decency, the stern need of sacrifice if we are to be saved.

The average American doesn't give a damn what the "Wall Street Bankers" say or think or do except when, as in the Nineteen Twenties, some of them sold us gilt-edged flypaper on which we were permanently stuck. You may be sure of this —not one shred of evidence has been produced to prove that Wilson's policy was at any time determined by our financial stake in the Allied cause. We do know that many bankers and businessmen were appeasement and profit minded then as some of them are now. Have you noted how our twitching and twittering "intellectuals" who have screamed at the late Neville Chamberlain as a "business" appeaser now advocate with their falsetto fury that we might possibly, maybe, perhaps slap Hitler lightly on the wrist but at all costs "stay at peace"?

It's perfectly true that some businessmen have been like the "camp followers" mentioned by Caesar and notorious in every war for picking up scraps of booty left by the victor. We have them today—the whisky speculators, the labor baiters, the Gestapo-minded men with soft hands and hard eyes, who would "make a deal" with Hitler if they could get away with it. That same sort gloated and grew fat on the profits made during

25

our neutrality from 1914 to 1917. They didn't want us in the war then. They don't now.

But most businessmen were patriots in 1917, as they are today, and had enough vision, let's say horse sense, to realize that business can be secure only in a society governed by laws and not by gangsters. So it may be that some of you who are businessmen actually did favor in 1917 the continuance of a system which, with all its defects and grievances, was still subject to a reign of law and the reasoned improvements of democracy rather than subject to Prussian militarism. You believed, as most of us did for a variety of reasons, that we should enter the war against the Kaiser's Germany. Most of you lost some big profits which you might have enjoyed—temporarily—if we had remained at peace. So today—there's "blood money" for you—temporarily—if we stay out. My guess is that as "hard-headed" men and as citizens just as decent and democratic as any of us you will prefer the high cost of suppressing international crime to the inevitable bankruptcy of succumbing to it.

As for the "Merchants of Death" who "led us" into the last war. Well, we know today what a cheap political scarecrow that is. Both our knowledge and common sense refuse to elevate the munitions manufacturers into gods of human destiny. They make their unpleasant goods and sell them because there are people (including us) who want them and will buy them. Occasionally some over-zealous salesman may have encouraged a Central American revolution, but to picture these practical gentlemen as playing a decisive role in the destinies of the world is plain silly. At the present moment, please note, we are grumbling because they are not working fast enough to suit our fancy and our need.

Nor did we fight to "pull England's chestnuts out of the fire." We never have. The propagandists who say we have done so cannot prove a single instance in our entire history as a nation to support their falsehood. And yet by using the Nazi-Communist technique of repeating a falsehood again and again they have deceived some honest, well-meaning folk and have soothed those frantic people who cannot bear to face the simple but sometimes hard truths of life. Have you observed how these same propagandists scream with rage because England is at moments reluctant to do the hard jobs of civilization which they urge us to shirk? Why doesn't England save Ethiopia or China or Austria or Czechoslovakia or Finland? I wonder how many of these propagandists urge us today to take our place beside Britain in the battle line of freedom.

Another popular narcotic which our propagandist historians and pseudo intellectuals have successfully peddled to many of us is so-called "Allied propaganda." They peddle this propaganda against propaganda on the assumption that Americans are a simple, childlike, almost moronic people who need nurses and guards to keep them out of mischief. It is insidious stuff, which, taken in too large doses, is likely to cause moral impotence and intellectual sterility. We are reminded of the old Quaker's remark to his wife, "All the world's mad except thee and me, and even thee art a little mad." We know why we fought, we can remember the big obvious facts which finally roused us to action and which our isolationist and pro-Nazi propagandists now try so frantically to obscure; we can search our hearts, our minds, and the written record, and we can honestly say that so-called "Allied propaganda" did not hasten by a day our entry into the last war.

America entered the last war for many reasons. Let's recall them briefly. It'll help keep our thinking straight.

The most immediate and compelling reason was simply that Germany, after repeated warnings and protests, continued to sink ships without warning, with a loss of American lives. If Germany had not sunk our ships and if American lives had not been lost in those actions, we probably would not have entered the war. The evidence is overwhelming on this point and it's on the record for all of us to see. It's true that the British blockade was at times annoying—although when we got in we were much tougher than our English cousins had been. (More about that later on.) But the killing of an American child counted more heavily with us than the seizure of a bale of cotton. The British irritated us, but we knew perfectly well that we would do the same—had done it more sternly during our Civil War. The Kaiser's government roused our righteous anger. Even so we were patient. Too patient, said some of our greatest statesmen like old T.R.—We can almost hear him now as he bitingly attacked Wilson's "notes, notes, notes" of protest against the German submarine warfare on our ships and our lives.

Well—the Kaiser then, like Hitler now, was mistaken about the American people. He counted, as Hitler does, on our isolationists and pacifists and those hand-wringing persons who whimper and do nothing. He thought we wouldn't fight and that if we did we wouldn't amount to much. Von Bernstorff, German ambassador in Washington, warned his government not to continue the U-boat warfare on us. To no avail. Finally the American people, the President, and our representatives in Congress made up their minds on that issue. If you have the time, I suggest that you again read Woodrow Wilson's superb War Message of April 2, 1917, and the speeches of those members of the House and Senate who voted for our entry into the war. You will remember with renewed pride why we fought. We clearly saw a tough fact and bravely met it.

With all our faults, we Americans nave a great faith in certain ideals—a faith that has moved mountains and has contributed mightily to our greatness as a nation. When Woodrow Wilson struck the moral note, the heart of America responded. Most Americans did believe that we were fighting "to make the world safe for democracy." Whether we succeeded or failed is irrelevant at this point. We did fight for something worth fighting for, and we need feel no regret or shame for that motive and purpose. Have you forgotten what Woodrow Wilson told us then and what I think he is telling us now?

It is a fearful thing to lead this great, peaceful people into war, into the most terrible and disastrous of all wars, civilization itself seeming to be in the balance.

But the right is more precious than peace, and we shall fight for the things which we have always carried nearest our hearts—for democracy, for the right of those who submit to authority to have a voice in their own Governments, for the rights and liberties of small nations, for a universal dominion of right by such a concert of free people as shall bring peace and safety to all nations and make the world itself at last free.

I am not ashamed of those words and those purposes—they are the very substance of the American spirit which Hitler and his clever allies in this country are now trying to kill. I am ashamed that, for a time, we repudiated those words, that we did not carry through, that we quit on the job, that we have listened for many years to the whines and screams of those who would drown out the still small voice of conscience and of warning. Well—today is another day. This time we won't fail. We'll do the job we once set out to do. You see, I am placing my bets—and advise you to do the same—on the moral traditions and the common sense of the American people.

Somewhat allied to the foregoing were our Anglo-Saxon heritage and traditions. English people and American people believe in their hearts that individual freedom is one of those few things worth fighting for and, if need be, worth dying for. It's true that most of us Americans of British ancestry do not feel it necessary to boast loudly of our heritage. We have gladly shared our Anglo-Saxon traditions of equal justice and ordered liberty with many fine peoples who came from other lands eager to enjoy our spiritual inheritance and our economic opportunities. Those traditions.

31

though often foolishly ignored or wickedly violated, are part of the fabric of our nation and our very lives. Magna Carta, the common law, the Bill of Rights, the King James Bible, the hymns of the Wesleys and Cardinal Newman, Shakespeare and Dickens, Mr. Valiant-for-Truth and Bobby Burns —they are the staples of our spiritual and mental life. They meant much to us in 1917. They mean more—they mean everything to us today because the danger to them is so much more terrible.

Time and isolationist propaganda may have dimmed some other reasons for our entry into the war, such as German militarism, Germany's support of Austria in July, 1914, the invasion of neutral Belgium, the introduction of poison gas, the dynamiting of our bridges and munition plants, the deportation and enslavement of Belgian civilians, the destruction of Louvain, and other brutal facts we could not ignore and should not forget.

But—"We won the war." Sure we did. Almost single-handed. Almost. Let's try to be honest with ourselves so that we may be fair to others. Let's remember what England and France and our other associates contributed to the winning of that war.

For instance, they fought the war for three years while we remained neutral and waxed rich at their expense. England, with a population one-third of ours, lost in dead alone nearly one million men; France, with a population less than one-third of ours, almost a million and a half; Canada, with a population less than New York State, about 100,000. As it was, we lost about 126,000. Remember that in citing these facts I'm simply suggesting that we be honest and fair.

We never knew the horror of an air raid, the terror and degradation of an invading army destroying our towns and cities and enslaving a large part of our civilian population to be hewers of wood and drawers of water in the enemy country. Fuel-less Sundays, Liberty Loan "drives," and one lump of sugar instead of two were among our major efforts. Yes, they helped—helped a lot, "turned the tide" and all that sort of thing. But as a nation we were spared the agony our comrades-in-arms endured.

And let's not forget that our fellow aemocracies supplied us with most of our artillery and nearly all our fighting planes; that of the five thousand antisubmarine craft operating in the submarine-infested waters we had only 160, or three per cent; that sixty per cent of our troops were transported by Britain and more than half our overseas army was convoyed by the British fleet. Yes—yes—our war effort was good enough and just in time. My point is that when we stop to think and make a real attempt to be fair about the relative measure of our war efforts and personal sacrifices the propaganda we have been fed for several years seems a bit indecent.

But they called America "Uncle Shylock"! Who did? Well, strangely enough, there have been some irresponsible politicians and journalists in England and France just as there are in this country. They aren't much help, often a damn nuisance, in solving a hard problem between friends—especially if one is a creditor and the other a debtor.

As a sensible person you will agree with me ("sensible" people nearly always agree with one) that the whole war debt problem was clumsily handled on both sides. Just to be fair, remember this—they didn't "hire the money"—we let them buy goods on credit (to keep them fighting while we got ready) and then, remember, we made it practically impossible for them to pay us back—thanks to our tariffs which shut out their goods. A wise banker, as distinct from a pawnbroker, does not keep his borrowers too poor to pay him. You're probably in too much of a hurry to rake over the ashes of this old problem—but please keep in mind one or two of the big facts I've mentioned. If you have any free time on your hands, you might read the speeches of our Senators when Congress authorized these loans—they gladly called them gifts then. But times change and memories are short. We know, however, that when gangsters are roaming the streets we shouldn't haggle over the price of a gun which our neighbor can use to good effect.

All right, you say, but what did we get out of the last war? Well—we kept the war from coming here by fighting it over there. That was something. We won a breathing spell of twenty years for democracy—others and our own. That's nothing to cry about. We prevented the German fleet from dominating the Atlantic. Not a bad result. We won the greatest chance in modern history to work for a secure and lasting peace—a chance which we ourselves proposed—a chance for a peace we might have enjoyed today. We killed it. You know how. Some Americans were a little tired, much frightened by their national maturity, and greatly confused by the clever isolationist propaganda of the time. So for twenty years we tried isolationism —and here we are today.

THE "CRIME OF VERSAILLES"

Long before Hitler made the "Crime of Versailles" his favorite bedtime story to the German people many of our "intellectuals" were talking and writing about it in the feverish manner of a town gossip. Pseudo historians, irresponsible journalists, and tired liberals who couldn't digest some of the rougher facts of life all did their bit. There was also some honest, intelligent, and justified criticism of it.

Not many of you have read even a small fraction of the Treaty of Versailles, and, in fact, very few of the loudest critics of the treaty have ever read it. I don't mean that our Pontius Pilate propagandists would behave any differently if they had read it because those people shun the sober truth like a pestilence. I mean they usually don't know what they're talking about but find it easy and congenial to repeat hearsay on hearsay—and too many of us lazily accept a good part of their tittle-tattle. We must admit, however, that as a treaty it had imperfections, having been drawn by imperfect men representing imperfect peoples, most of whom for four years had endured a war that was not exactly perfect.

There's this and that and a thousand and one other things to be said about the "Crime of Versailles." I merely want to suggest a few things to remember.

Alsace-Lorraine was restored to France. Any objections? The house hears none.

Germany lost some colonies in Africa. You've heard a great "hue and cry" about these "lost colonies" as if they were Germany's breadbasket. Actually, in 1913, they accounted for less than one-half of 1 per cent of her foreign trade. They lack most of her essential needs in raw materials. As for "living space"—well there was no mad rush by Germans to live in them. We know that there were more Germans living in the city of Paris in 1913 than in all Germany's African colonies. And don't forget that the Nazis want these colonies as closed preserves—sources of military supplies— rather than open to world trade under the mandate system set up by the Versailles Treaty. This "crybaby" demand of German propaganda is revolting to those of us who take the trouble to see what lies behind it, but it has a strong appeal to shallow sentimentalists in this country.

What, you ask, is behind all this "crybaby" talk? That's simple. Have you read *Mein Kampf* and Hitler's and Goebbel's latest speeches? Hitler has told us that it would be "insane folly" for the Nazis to fight merely to restore Germany's 1914 boundaries. The "crybaby" propaganda is merely a smoke screen to befuddle us.

Then there were the reparations. Much too much. Trivial, though, according to the standards the Germans set when they are in the saddle. At any rate, machinery was set up whereby the payments could be scaled down to a reasonable figure and that was shortly done. As we shall soon see, Germany's "burden" after the war was not the cost of the reparations but of the war itself— a great big fact which the Nazis and their allies in this country never, never mention. Meanwhile, you might scratch your heads and recall why and for what the reparations were asked. I'll leave that for you to figure out.

Crocodile tears have been shed over the "war guilt clause." The Beard type of propagandist and some queer footnote minds in our colleges have tried to smudge a pretty definite record. Through all the fog and smoke of controversy some things are clear. England and France did not invade neutral Belgium. Germany did. The war was not fought on German soil. We know what the Prussian militarists wanted. We remember that Austria-Hungary started the fight in July, 1914, and that Germany backed her up. If you're interested enough to go into it, you might read the minutes of the Austro-Hungarian Cabinet meeting of July 7, 1914—they'll clear your head of the "sob sister stories" peddled by Hitler, the Beards, and our pseudo intellectuals.

"But—but—the Germans are a proud people." Since when has such pride become a cardinal and cleansing virtue? And incidentally, just what sort of things do they take pride in? While we're about it, let's make an honest, clear-cut distinction in our minds between the German liberal in the concentration camps and Himmler's Gestapo, between our pleasant, peaceful "music-loving" neighbor of German ancestry and the great sodden mass of Germans in Germany who will support Hitler until we thrash them. You can't beat a *panzer* division with a lollipop.

Mind you, the Treaty of Versailles was imperfect. France made some mistakes. Britain made some. America made some. I think the Polish settlement creating the "corridor"—the least defensible part of the treaty—was the brain child of the American delegation. Some heartbreaking decisions had to be made and were made. There were errors of judgment and defects of vision. It is honorable and wise and morally healthy that we should see such errors and defects and, more important, do our full share in correcting them. Sound criticism is essential to progress in a democracy. (This letter is no "paean of praise.") But our enemies inside and outside of America have tried to magnify and pervert honest criticism into an excuse for a defense of the basest crimes against democracy itself—into a weapon that would destroy the very freedom of mind which encourages such criticism. So, when you look back at our mistakes, don't grow maudlin. We'll make plenty more. Our faith is, however, that democracy will keep on trying to win the just, the humane, the right things of life.

We can say this about what Hitler calls the "Crime of Versailles"—there has been no other major treaty in modern history, concluded between nations formerly at war, in which moral values, high principles, and honest work played so great and in many instances so decisive a part as in the Treaty of Versailles. Maybe it would have been better if America and the Allies had drawn a cold-blooded treaty of terrible revenge with no "nonsense" and fancy ideas about international law and justice and respect for the opinions of mankind. Maybe it would have been better. But it just wasn't that kind of treaty. I suppose the reason is that free men, however often they may falter and fail, simply refused then as they refuse now (despite all Hitler's efforts) to retrace the long, hard road from the jungle. Somehow, democracy pushes ahead.

There was one magnificent attempt in the Versailles Treaty for a better world—the League of Nations. Our President, Woodrow Wilson, fought hard for it. France yielded many demands for her security because of it. Those awful European nations, our recent associates, accepted it. America turned it down. We wanted to preach, not work, for a world of peace and ordered liberty. America stumbled and fell. So we must sacrifice all the more in this war and really work to keep the peace we must earn. Woodrow Wilson will yet win his fight. The Unknown Soldier did not die in vain.

Do you remember what the German leaders said they were going to do to the rest of the world if they won? If you don't and are really interested, I suggest that you dig back into the official documents and newspaper files of twenty-five years ago and also read the treaty of Brest-Litovsk. The isolationist and pro-Nazi propagandists today will not tell you, nor will the facing-both-ways columnists. Most of them know, however, that had Germany won, the Treaty of Versailles, in comparison with the German peace terms, would have seemed like the Sermon on the Mount. You will recall that the treaty of Brest-Litovsk ended Russia's part in the last war. A detailed analysis of it is not possible in this letter, but suffice it to say that Germany took from Russia more than a third of her population, 32 per cent of her agricultural land, more than half her industries, and about 90

41

per cent of her coal mines. When Germany crushed Rumania in the last war, an even more terrible treaty was forced down her throat—the Peace of Bucharest.

Those treaties were merely mild examples of Prussian militarism. Put them on a convenient shelf in your minds for handy reference in the future. And remember that although German militarism has now sunk under the Nazis to the lowest depravity known to history it was a brutal menace to democracy when we fought and temporarily checked it twenty-three years ago.

WASTED YEARS

When we pause to look backward and think quietly about the past, we regret something more than our big mistakes, heavy losses, sharp defeats, and thwarted hopes—we regret the time we've wasted. I'm not speaking about those insufferably perfect people who never waste a moment. I don't mean the time that is part of a well-earned rest—I mean the time when we know we should have been on the job, working for the things we want most. So it was with the great democracies—America, Britain, and France—from 1919 to 1939. Those were wasted years. Tragically wasted. Peace based on law and backed with power could have been firmly established. But they threw the chance away by wishing and dreaming and hoping—not working for it. And let us Americans be manly enough to stop prattling about how wonderful we are and honestly admit that our fault was as great as any other's. Greater, really, because we added insult to injury by boasting to high heaven of our virtues.

While we wasted those twenty years, what did we do? We duped ourselves with fantastic nonsense about poor Germany's postwar years, and we did nothing to save the peace for which we fought—except to give and drop in on some very pretty but utterly futile international tea parties. Let's take a quick, clear look backward. We can profit by it now and in the coming years.

During those twenty years Germany, with the frantic aid of some self-styled "liberals" in America, won the greatest triumph in the history of propaganda—the poisonous effects of which we can still see and smell. They sold us a vast quantity of "bootleg" goods on foreign affairs, and some people are showing today the distasteful aftereffects of taking too much. Hitlerism was such a vile dose that many people stopped dealing with certain "intellectual" bootleggers and racketeers among our professors and writers so that they have clear heads today. But poisons linger longer in the mind than in the body—a fact which our isolationist and pro-Nazi propagandists well know. I'm talking about the immensely successful lies regarding postwar Germany. You know—all the sentimental slush about how harshly Germany was treated and how terribly she suffered and that such treatment and suffering explain and even excuse her present bestiality under the Nazis. Some people have stayed roaring drunk on that stuff for years.

What are the facts?

44

Let's see. Suppose we look briefly into the whining propaganda about Germany's sufferings under the British blockade. It's well to do so especially as we have recently heard the sobs of our appeasers and American Nazis—sobs about the present blockade—sobs, I'm glad to say, which did not deceive us.

The blockade in the last war was very effective in defeating Prussian militarism. That fact alone has naturally caused our pro-Nazi, anti-British propagandists much anguish. When the United States entered the war, the blockade was made even more effective. We were tougher than the British in enforcing it. Please remember that. And we'll be just as tough after we enter this war. When the Germans decide they'd rather make butter than guns, that they'd rather eat than kill, the war will end. Not till then.

Yes, the blockade was continued after the actual fighting stopped, but its restrictions were removed about nine months before the Treaty of Versailles was ratified and peace actually established. If you took the trouble to dig into history, you would discover other facts, such as: that the delay in removing the blockade restrictions was caused by the German refusal for months to deliver the ships needed to transport food supplies and gold to pay for them; that the British were the first to propose lifting the blockade; and that Germany's food shortage was actually worse for a time after it was lifted. Incidentally, very incidentally, although the German people suffered, so did some other people—people whose fields had been ruined, whose houses had been pillaged and blown to bits, and whose towns and cities had been plundered by the Prussian invaders—people who were on our side.

Now then—let's discuss "Germany's postwar burden" about which some good sense and much drool and drivel have been said and written. The one great big fact about that "burden" is simply this—it was relatively light. Yes—compared with the burden carried by the English and French peoples after the war it was very light. And as regards the so-called financial "servitudes" of the Versailles Treaty it was a little burden indeed and in a few years it became no burden at all. Then why all the hubbub? Partly because the German whine in defeat is as tremendous as Germany's cruelty in victory. Partly because, under Hitler, it's a method to throw dust in our eyes. Partly because our Pontius Pilate propagandists don't want you to know the facts. And partly because the plain hard truth makes our pseudo intellectuals almost hysterical so that they quite naturally steer clear of it whenever possible.

All right, you say, let's have the facts.

Germany's postwar burden was really the cost of

the war itself. It's true that the German government paid a certain amount in reparations—about one-fourth the cost of her war efforts. The balance sheet shows, however, that what Germany actually paid out was more than offset by the amounts paid into Germany by foreign investors, mostly American and British. So the only burden on German finances was the nation's war costs. (It is a tragic irony that the money invested in Germany to put her "on her feet" was the means whereby she has enslaved most of Europe and to-day menaces everything we hold dear. We must remember that.)

And stick this in your mind—the tax burden "per head" after the war was far greater in England, France, and the United States than in Germany. In England in 1923-4, for example, the citizen was paying about four times as much in taxes as the German citizen was paying. The Germans simply did not try, as Britain and America did, to meet their bills and put their house in order. It was so much easier to whine. We must admit that with the aid of our own ignorant or unscrupulous sentimentalists the whines had a sickening success both here and inside Germany.

The German people deliberately refused to face the truth that it was the war itself and their historic militarism which had cost them dear. They loved their vast army—it was the very soul of the nation. So a fantastic lie and a dramatic fiction were invented to sustain their faith in the army and their lust for power over other peoples. The lie was the so-called "dagger thrust in the back" inflicted by the Socialists (Hitler later added the Jews). It's clearly on the record that the Socialists and organized labor backed the German government to the end and that Ludendorff and the other German generals knew their army was beaten. The fiction was the "Crime of Versailles," which helped the Germans forget that the war and their long lust for militarism had caused their troubles and hardships.

We can understand why the German people indulged in this frightful self-deception. Their political standards and experience were utterly different from those of England and the United States. They never knew the meaning of democracy or that slow but steady growth of freedom under the law which is the chief characteristic of Anglo-Saxon civilization. Serfdom existed in Germany well into the nineteenth century. Self-government—that most difficult and, we think, most worth-while form of government—they did not understand and barely endured for fourteen years under the Weimar Republic. The old chancellor, Prince von Bülow, said truly enough, "We are not a political people." They simply prefer obedience to liberty and power to law. What they wanted was most certainly not the grim, plain truth which would set them free—a frightening prospect—but scapegoats and fictions which would soothe their wounded pride and a leader whom they could obey in a mad quest for power. Hitler gave them what they wanted. He's their man and don't forget it. Exceptions—magnificent exceptions—yes. They have fled to other lands or are dying under torture in the concentration camps.

Yes—we can understand the morbid self-pity of the German people after the last war and their failure to come to grips honestly, patiently, and wholeheartedly with the real causes of their unhappiness. It is much more difficult to understand, probably only a pathologist can explain the self-styled "liberals" in this country who deliberately refused to see or hear the plain facts of Germany's relatively light postwar burden, who blinded themselves to the historic and living menace of German militarism, and who gave frenzied aid to the very forces of self-delusion in Germany which made Hitler possible even after the Weimar Republic had removed every last one of the so-called "economic servitudes" of the Versailles Treaty. Well—Hitler is their man, too.

During those wasted years, 1919-1939, certain unscrupulous politicians and propagandists worked hard, day in and day out, to isolate and imperil

America. They've done it. That sort of person costs our democracy too much.

But didn't we tell the world that peace was wonderful and that we liked it very much? Yes. Exactly that and no more. We certainly did talk and talk. Criticized, preached, exhorted, declaimed, prayed, and moaned. And did nothing. Through it all we felt a lurking shame because we had quit on the hard job and had timidly thrown away the superb opportunity our President, Woodrow Wilson, had given the world. To hide our shame we put on the shabby robe of self-righteousness, went to a few international conferences, slinked into an "unofficial observer's" seat at the League of Nations meetings and complained because Britain didn't do this, that, and the other thing to keep us and the rest of the world completely soft and warm and comfortable. You say there's no use crying over spilled milk. That's right. And yet—and yet because we spilled too much milk then blood is being spilled now.

Do you remember the Washington Arms Conference in 1921? There were some unusually pretty speeches made at that affair. One worth-while bit of statesmanship was achieved, thanks to the efforts of Arthur Meighen, Canada's great Prime Minister at the time. England and Japan had an alliance, and Mr. Meighen, acutely aware of its possible future embarrassment to the English-speaking nations, urged British statesmen to cut loose from it. That was deftly done by the late Lord Balfour, and the Nine Power Treaty, a toothless statement of good intentions, was substituted to save Japan's face and to give China a pathetic hope of future territorial security. There was also a proposal, unanimously adopted, to save the world with arithmetic. It was so nice and simple—the big naval powers agreed to maintain their capital ship strength at the ratio of "five-five-three." France was bitterly denounced by some of our intellectuals as being "militaristic" because Briand expressed fear that Germany might again rearm and threaten the peace and freedom of the world. But the Conference ended happily if a bit stuffily with a bumbling speech by Warren G. Harding.

Oh, of course, there were some other "conferences" where we piddled and frittered time away and made sure that whatever we might say or preach we would never, never show or accept any sense of "obligation" as a great and manly democracy in the family of nations. This piddle and fritter foreign policy had a kind of Valentine Day party at the time of the Kellogg-Briand "peace pact." There were sugar and spice and everything that's nice. War was bravely, solemnly "renounced." No "commitments," no "pledges," no "obligations," no work. Nothing.

And let us give the tribute of a sigh to that respectable and potentially useful organization—the World Court. The fatal weakness of it was the lack of a policeman to carry out its decisions. Even with that weakness it still retained a tinge of moral authority which dismayed our isolationists. True, our presidents, Messrs. Harding, Coolidge, and Hoover (when you start to criticize old Chamberlain, remember them)—those gentlemen recommended it with about as much enthusiasm as an Episcopalian vicar describes the Presbyterian minister on the next block. But the Congress of the United States had swerved from Woodrow Wilson to the isolationist propagandists and rejected even that symbolic attempt to establish peace based on law. Just in passing, I want to point out again that the World Court, worthy as it was, could not by itself have established and maintained a reign of law among the nations. The reason is clear. We need the policeman's club as well as the judge's robe to keep the peace. You and I know that. The pseudo intellectual never will.

In the Nineteen Thirties the attitude of many Americans on foreign affairs expanded rapidly from piddle and fritter to piddle, fritter, and fuss. The falsetto cries of our emasculated intellectuals grew louder and shriller as they urged the *other* democracies to *do* something about China, about Ethiopia, about Spain, about Austria, about Czechoslovakia. The hissings of anti-British and pro-

Nazi propagandists sickened the air and soiled the printed page. Hitler counted on them. They served him well. Hitler counted on our isolationists. They did not fail him. In France his propaganda weakened the people's powers of resistance, in England it put most of the nation's leaders to sleep, in America it made the Congress of the United States scuttle and run.

Munich and "appeasement." Yes—Mr. Chamberlain, with a gun at his head, yielded. Then, like a certain type of narrow-minded businessman (honorable in his dealings and blind in his understanding even of his own best interests)—then he almost persuaded himself that everything would work out for the best. Then, when his illusions were torn to shreds, he met the Nazi criminal bravely but wearily, honestly but inadequately. America did not do even that. She talked and talked, and screamed and preached, looked and ran away under the leadership of the isolationist propagandists just as Hitler expected and wanted her to do.

At this point, let's indulge for a moment in a little speculation—not entirely idle speculation because it might help us in the better days to come. Let's suppose that after Munich the great democracies of the world—America, the British Commonwealth of Nations, France, and the smaller countries of Scandinavia and Holland and Belgium—and our South American neighbors—let's

53

suppose they had gathered together and said: "We want peace and we'll work for it. We want our own way of life, neighborly good will, religious tolerance, personal freedom, democracy which with all its faults and failures and blunders and sins can assure us the prizes of the future while keeping strong and useful the worthy and hard-won rewards of our past. We want these things for ourselves and our children enough to fight and kill and die for them. We shall stick together through thick and thin, come what may." I think if they had said that—and meant it—the Nazis would not have moved, there would have been no war. True, it's a guess. But remember that the Germans, whether ruled by a kaiser or a führer, worship definitely superior power and the will to use it to the limit. Yes, it's a guess. Much worse— it's a "might-have-been." But it will come to pass.

America could have made those words possible. There were not a sufficient number of us wise enough and willing enough at the time to make our government do it. No—American democracy failed again. Too many of us, blinded and deafened by pro-Nazi and isolationist propaganda, desperately chanted, "Peace—it's wonderful," and shamefacedly muttered, "Let England do it."

During that year from Munich to the outbreak of the war, when the free democracies lost their great chance for peace—and even up to now—

false sentimentality—not righteous sentiment—false sentimentality (our most dangerous national vice) threatened the basic manliness of American character. We have been gushingly told again and again and again that our resources are "boundless," our strength is "boundless," our courage is "boundless," our heroism is "boundless," our idealism is "boundless," our love of freedom and justice and democracy is "boundless." So is gas.

If bitter criticism of our brother democracies and sugary praise of ourselves could make a better world, we would have succeeded long ago. But a better world is not made that way. Self-coddling, running away, wishful thinking did not make us great and useful. And they will not save us. "Faith without works is dead." You and I know that. Thank God we know it in time to act—in the nick of time.

It seems almost as incredible and certainly as horrible as a nightmare that during the spring and summer months of 1939 our Pontius Pilate isolationists in Congress, the pulpit, and the classroom kept shouting "there will be no war," kept telling us to "follow the example" of "neutral" Holland, "neutral" Norway, "neutral" Finland and so on, kept hysterically shrieking "warmonger" at those who saw and warned us of the looming Nazi menace. Look at those Pontius Pilates and mark them well. They bear an unmistakable and unforgettable stain.

We are asked to shut our eyes to the most blazing truths, to avert our gaze from the plain facts of our contemporary life, to stuff our ears and to harden our hearts so that somehow, in some way, we can escape from the tough realities of this world and, as a nation, evade the tasks which nature, our moral traditions, and the uncompromising forces of destiny have set for us to do.

And so the cries of our Pontius Pilates grow more and more shrill as we pay them less and less attention. But they can still do us harm. So note them well. They are in the active service, consciously or unconsciously, of Adolf Hitler and his Huns.

Now that we are cutting loose from the dead weight of timidity and shame of those wasted years, 1919-1939, now that we are manfully facing the truth, now that we are casting out of our minds and hearts the vile teachings of our morally impotent intellectuals, now that we again fear God and are about to do our part, we shall be once more a truly happy, a truly brave, a truly free, a truly good people.

HITLER'S BLITZKRIEG IN AMERICA

Among Hitler's major triumphs in the war so far have been those over the mind and spirit of America. Our neutrality was his greatest hope—his very best chance to win. He and his gangsters knew it, and they have used the same technique with us as they have done with others—to bore from within and with the frantic aid of kindred spirits, of milksop intellectuals and demagogic politicians to weaken our will to think and to act. The Nazis coolly calculated that if they could soften the mind and soul of America, if they could somehow keep us nervously impotent—somehow keep us neutral—they would enslave the world. Their success up to now has been almost miraculous when we stop to look at the record: Hitler's own words telling us in the plainest way his whole technique of lies and treachery, his open violation of every pledge made to other nations, his bold and sickening use of terror and force.

It's true that now—in the nick of time that a patient God has given us—we are pulling ourselves together and are preparing to do our part as a law-abiding neighbor to rid the world of the Nazi gangsters. But we have just begun. Let's again briefly study Hitler's past so that we can see what we're up against, so that we can crush ruthlessly the enemies within our gates, so that in our hard march to victory we may avoid the tricks and traps the Nazis and their allies in this country will set in our path.

Perhaps the most important thing for you to remember is simply this—at no time, under no circumstances, and no matter what he says can you take the word—believe the promise—of Herr Hitler. If you do, you may die. In *Mein Kampf* he has told you plainly, so that there is no possible excuse for not understanding, his complete faith in the power of the lie. He said: "The masses will fall victims to a big lie more readily than to a small one, for they themselves only tell small lies, being ashamed to tell big ones. Untruthfulness on a large scale does not occur to them, and they do not believe in the possibility of such amazing impudence, such scandalous falsification, on the part of others. Some part of even the most glaring lie will always remain behind . . . ." He has also described exactly how he destroys: "Conceal your real intentions; conciliate your strongest opponents by pretending that you are on their side; gradually increase the strength of your position by tactical advances, each one of which is not vital enough to arouse serious opposition but the sum of which enormously add to your power; and then, at the given moment, throw down the mask and launch a mass attack upon your enemies." The knaves or fools among our Congressional isolationists try to make you forget or simply ignore those words. That is one reason why Hitler has counted on them to keep us out of war.

Look once again at his record of broken pledges —so criminally fantastic that the mind of an ordinary decent man can hardly take it in. But here it is in a nutshell from February 10, 1933, to October 6, 1939:

Berlin, February 10, 1933.
The first and best point of the Government's program is that we won't lie and we won't swindle.

Berlin, May 17, 1933.
The German Government wish to settle all difficult questions with other governments by peaceful methods. They know that any military action in Europe, even if completely successful, would, in view of the sacrifice, bear no relation to the profit to be obtained. . . .

Germany will tread no other path than that laid down by the Treaties. *The German Government will discuss all political and economic questions only within the framework of, and through, the Treaties.*

The German people have no thought of invading any country.

On the radio, May 27, 1933.
We do not want a war merely for the purpose of bringing to Germany people who simply do not want to be, or cannot be, Germans.

On October 14, Germany left the League of Nations.

Berlin, November 10, 1933.
I am not crazy enough to want a war. . . .
When has the German people ever broken its word?

Berlin, January 13, 1934.
The assertion that the German Reich plans to coerce the Austrian State is absurd and cannot be substantiated or proved. . . .

After the Saar question has been settled, the German Government is ready to accept not only the letter but the spirit of the Locarno Pact. . . .

Hamburg, August 17, 1934.
The German Government, like the German people, are filled with the unconditional wish to make the greatest possible contribution to the preservation of peace in this world.

On May 16, 1935, Germany announced conscription.

Berlin, May 21, 1935.

The German Government intend not to sign any treaty which seems to them incapable of fulfillment, but will scrupulously observe every treaty voluntarily concluded, even if it was drawn up before their assumption of power and office....

Germany has concluded a non-aggression pact with Poland, which is more than a valuable contribution to European peace, and she will adhere to it unconditionally.... We recognize the Polish State as the home of a great patriotic nation with the understanding and the cordial friendship of candid nationalists.

Germany neither intends nor wishes to interfere in the internal affairs of Austria, to annex Austria, or to conclude an Anschluss.

On March 7, Germany reoccupied the Rhineland and denounced Locarno.

Berlin, March 7, 1936.

We have no territorial demands to make in Europe.

Munich, March 15, 1936.

The German people do not wish to continue waging war to readjust frontiers.

Berlin, May 1, 1936.

The lie goes forth again that Germany tomor-

row or the day after will fall upon Austria or Czechoslovakia.

Berlin, January 30, 1937.

I do not want to leave any doubt as to the following: We look upon Bolshevism as upon an intolerable danger to the world.... For this it is necessary that we should avoid all close contacts with the bearers of these poisonous bacilli.... Any treaty links between Germany and present-day Bolshevist Russia would be without any value whatsoever....

Berlin, February 20, 1938.

Shall I remind you of the Bolshevist Revolution which slaughtered millions upon millions of people, but whose blood-stained murderers still occupy high places? ... With one single country alone we have detested to enter into relationships. That state is Soviet Russia.

The Polish State respects the national conditions in this country, and Danzig and Germany respect Polish rights. Thus it has been possible to find the way to an understanding which, emanating from Danzig, in spite of the assertions of many mischief-makers, has succeeded in removing all friction between Germany and Poland, and made it possible to work together in true amity.

On March 11, Germany invaded Austria.

Berlin, May 1, 1938.

The motto must be, never war again.

Berlin, September 26, 1938.

We have assured all our immediate neighbors of the integrity of their territory so far as Germany is concerned. That is no hollow phrase; it is our sacred will. . . .

The Sudetenland is the last territorial claim which I have to make in Europe. . . . I have assured Mr. Chamberlain, and I emphasize it now, that when this problem is solved, Germany has no more territorial problems in Europe.

Saarbrucken, October 9, 1938.

Now as a strong State, we can be ready to pursue a policy of understanding with surrounding states. We want nothing from them. We have no wishes or demands; we desire peace. . . .

Berchtesgaden, January 1, 1939.

In general we have but one wish—that in the coming year we may be able to make our contribution to this general pacification of the whole world.

Berlin, January 30, 1939.

Only the warmongers think there will be a war. I think there will be a long period of peace.

On March 15, Germany seized Czechoslovakia and on March 21, annexed Memel.

Berlin, April 28, 1939.

Mr. Roosevelt believes *that the "tide of events" is once more bringing the threat of arms, and that if this threat of arms continues, a large part of the world is condemned to a common ruin. As far as Germany is concerned, I know nothing of this kind of threat to other nations.*

On August 21, Germany signed a pact with Russia and on September 1, invaded Poland.

Berlin, September 1, 1939.

I will not war against women and children. I have ordered my air force to restrict itself to attacks on military objectives.

The bombing of Polish open towns began on the first day of the war and on September 3, the *Athenia* was sunk. *You know what has happened since.*

Berlin, October 6, 1939.

And I personally take exception at seeing foreign statesmen stand up and call me guilty of having broken my word....

You and I know that on the basis of his words and his works we can never, never make peace with Hitler and the gangsters and perverts around him. Some of our Pontius Pilate propagandists know it in their hearts and for certain horrible reasons won't tell you. Likewise, some demagogues

64

and shifty politicians in and out of Congress. There are also, of course, many sugary sentimentalists who don't know it. Hitler counted on all of them to help him destroy us English-speaking peoples. He was so sure of our moral decadence—so sure we would not fight. Several years ago he told a friend, "There will be no new Wilson arising to stir up America against us."

Hitler has scored many triumphs in his blitzkrieg against the nerve centers of the American people. Let's count the casualties which he and our isolationist propagandists have inflicted on America. It's not a pleasant task. But it's part of the job we have to do for ourselves and our children. We Americans must have clear heads and clean hearts to fight freedom's greatest battle.

When, in September, 1939, Hitler started the war for which he and the Germans had so carefully and sacrificially prepared, what happened inside America? Well—in fear of Hitler and of having to do anything to check his barbarians, the Congress of the United States hauled down the American flag over a great part of the waters of the world and adopted the policy of "scuttle and run." I think that future generations of Americans will read that page in our history with a hot flush of shame. To his lasting honor, the greatest statesman in the American Senate, Carter Glass of Virginia, denounced this action as taking the

United States "to the verge of poltroonism" and as dishonoring our World War dead.

When, in the early months of the war, the Germans shot schoolboys in Prague as an example to other children, when they murdered Catholic priests and tortured and enslaved the inhabitants of Poland, when they threatened the same treatment to the helpless people of Norway and Sweden if they permitted an Allied army to aid Finland, there were, here and there, nervous whispers of regret. But, when the British navy delayed our ships several hours, as it had a right to do under international law, Hitler's friends among our Congressmen and intellectuals shrieked with rage.

Finland? Ah yes—"gallant little Finland." What did we do? We wrung our hands. Anything else? Indeed yes. The Congress of the mightiest single democracy on earth, after eight weeks of hysterical indecision, finally approved a bill whereby Finland was loaned a little money to buy, if she wished, coffins to bury her dead but not arms with which to defend her liberty. So great was the hysteria of Congress that Finland's name did not even appear in that magnificent gesture of the American Republic. But our pro-Nazi and anti-British isolationists obscenely mocked at England and France because they did not send a large army to Finland's aid, which, as the Finnish leaders said, Norway and Sweden would not permit.

Have you forgotten the sly murmurings of some gutter minds among our isolationists about this being a "phony war" and a "struggle between rival imperialisms" and "they're all alike." Many very decent-minded people were trapped—temporarily—by that talk. But the real culprits who still repeat some of those phrases—mark them well, I say, for they are working Hitler's will; they are enemies of the Republic.

When the Nazis took over Denmark and Norway, most of us felt disgust and righteous anger. But certain people sat up and exclaimed, "Thank heavens, the war is getting really interesting." And others, the anti-British and pro-Nazis, gleefully pointed out that Germany had again shown such masterly efficiency and contemptuously asked why Britain had not seized them first, knowing full well that she was finally fighting, among other things, to stop the cold-blooded murder of small nations. Denmark and Norway, remember, were among those snug, harmless, decent peoples whose policy of neutrality our isolationists had begged us to follow.

That was last April. We were not facing the facts because, as a nation, we were still stupefied by the popular narcotics fed us by the Beard-like intellectuals, still hypnotized by the anti-British and pro-Nazi propaganda. Also, the world then, as it seems to us now, was very different. The innocent peoples of Holland and Belgium still cultivated their gardens in the twilight of a peaceful if precarious neutrality. The flag of Liberty, Equality, and Fraternity still waved proudly and serenely over the most civilized nation on the European Continent. War, many innocent Americans thought, was of course a terrible thing, but as wars go it would be a comfortable one; we could all settle down very snug and safe behind the Maginot Line and the British fleet and wait until the German army got tired of the war, or the "kindly" German people revolted against their hated masters, or Hitler fell downstairs and broke his neck, or something else happened that would end it all very nicely. So we lived in a fairyland of wishful thinking which adults seem to crave as much as children when reality gets tough.

Well—last May—you know what happened. Holland conquered with almost incredible cruelty. Belgium crushed. Suddenly there was no Maginot Line. Paris, the "City of Light," in the hands of the barbarians. America became alarmed.

Let it never be forgotten how magnificently this "home of the brave" rose to the occasion. We talked more than ever; we wept; we wrung our hands. When France made her dying appeal to us, what did we do? We warmheartedly assured her, in effect, that we would redouble our efforts to sell to her for cash down and at a nice profit, just as fast and as soon as we could, the war supplies she might want. Strange as it may seem, that was not quite enough to help her carry on. (Incidentally, did you know that at Yorktown in 1781 there were more French soldiers and sailors than Americans?) Oh yes, Congress hastily appropriated billions and billions of dollars for defense—for a "two-ocean navy" which, if the Axis powers destroyed England, they would of course give us six or seven years to build.

And yet there were signs of a moral awakening among most Americans. Dunkerque helped. "A colossal military disaster." True. But also an answer to the prayers of liberty-loving men and women throughout the world. In that night of defeat and disaster a tiny star of faith and hope was born. England could "take it" as she had always done. Most of us began once again to feel like Americans. Free men still knew how to fight for freedom. Our truly liberal spirits in the colleges, the professions, among labor leaders and in business, who had been drowsing, put aside their illusions and wishful thinking and spoke out clear and bold. We began slowly and confusedly, it's true—but surely—to throw off the poisonous propaganda we had been fed by our whining pseudo intellectuals, the Pontius Pilate politicians, the Fascist and Communist isolationists, the hysterical pacifists, and all those "passive barbarians" in our midst who give a fawning acquiescence to ruthless power. Many of you knew as a matter of plain decency and hard sense that we must help the rest of our neighbors in the English-speaking world.

Yes—it was only a beginning. The recovery of all that is manliest in the American character and tradition was slow—fearfully slow. Our enemies outside and inside America redoubled their efforts to stop it. A few knaves in our midst were, as is always the case, aided and abetted by a larger number of fools. We were still jabbering and did very little. True, we sold to the British some old, second-hand army rifles for cash down. Then there was the destroyer-naval-base deal. That was good. But the effects of isolationist and anti-British propaganda were still so vicious that it was evidently thought wise to make it appear as a horse trade in which we got the better of the one other great democracy left in the world—while she was fighting for life. However, that aspect of the trade did not rest well on the consciences of many Americans.

The presidential campaign checked somewhat our slow progress toward honest thought and real work. But let's skip it.

During last summer and fall, self-deception still held a dominant if diminishing influence in our thinking. You know what I mean. All the piffle and puff to the effect that "we really are in the war" and "we can help Britain more by staying out" and "we're doing all we can—what more can we do." We knew damn well that was bunk. But it isn't easy to throw off twenty years of lying propaganda—especially when it has been vastly increased and efficiently directed by the Nazi machine.

Pontius Pilate knew, however, that he was in danger. He saw that Uncle Sam was waking up and looking at him with a quizzical and rather cold eye. So he beat a strategic retreat and joined lustily in our last great attempt at national self-deception—"Short of War." Aid to our friends and kinsmen of the English-speaking world? Yes—yes, of course. But not too much. And for cash down. And at no risk to ourselves. We might want to make a deal with Hitler some day. Take it easy. Maybe Britain will lose anyway. Maybe Britain will win anyway. Go slow—slow—slow. Today that is Hitler's last great hope—that America will go slow.

"Short of war." Many fine Americans who detest Nazism used that phrase in a defensive spirit. The Nazi and isolationist propaganda had been so successful over such a long period that they feared the jibes and jeers of the Pontius Pilates in our midst. Quite a few honestly thought that it would at least be wise to do something, though relatively trivial, while hoping and waiting to do more. There were other citizens who simply and eagerly fooled themselves with one of the most ancient and everlasting follies of mankind—the belief that a maximum of good can be achieved by a minimum of effort—the "eat your cake and have it, too" philosophy which always appeals to the adolescent mind.

"Short of war." But we began to realize last summer and know now that if Britain doesn't win we shall be in a last ditch fight for life—and utterly alone. Britain, in fighting for her life, is also fighting the battle of world freedom and world democracy. And yet the Pontius Pilates cry, "Sell if you can, lend if you must, fight never." America is in the gravest danger since the first English settlers landed at Jamestown and Plymouth. But, we are told, we must not fight until we're alone—we must not fight while all the rest of the English-speaking peoples are fighting and can be our allies. Only if and when they are beaten down then—then we'll fight like—like what? Rats in a corner? Then—pray tell—what will be *our* "war aims"? "Whom the gods would destroy, they first make mad." Our enemies know that and they urge, preach, scream, and whisper with an infinite variety of words the deathly doctrine of the "cornered rat." And the supreme tragedy is that good men aid them knowing not what they do.

"Short of war." Men once said other things in times that tried their souls—in times not quite so desperate as today. Men once said, "Give me liberty or give me death." Men once said: "Fondly do we hope—fervently do we pray—that this mighty scourge of war may speedily pass away. Yet if God wills that it continue until ... every drop of blood drawn with the lash shall be paid by another, drawn with the sword, as was said three thousand years ago, so still it must be said: 'The judgments of the Lord are true and righteous altogether.'" Men once said: "There is, therefore, but one response possible from us: Force, force to the utmost, Force without stint or limit, the righteous and triumphant Force which shall make Right the law of the world, and cast every selfish dominion down in the dust."

"Short of war"? No. Not much longer. We are decent men and women. Hitler's blitzkriegs and threats and propaganda are terrific, but the character of the American people is more.

BRITAIN AND AMERICA:
OLD GRUDGES AND NEW LIES

I suppose most of you have seen from time to time some pathetic people who suffer from an acute sense of inferiority. I don't mean the true humility of mind and spirit—one of the supreme and lesser known human virtues. You know what I mean—the fellow who lacks steady values and fears himself and therefore frantically seeks some kind of self-assurance by displaying a groveling servility or a malicious envy toward something he would like to be but cannot. That kind of man, we know, is abnormal. He is usually a nuisance but at times a menace. Hitler is of course the perfect example. And today, here in America, he is served consciously or unconsciously by two other unpleasant types—the Anglophile and the Anglophobe.

The Anglophile is a nuisance and the Anglophobe a menace. We can dispose of the nuisance in a few words. I have seen with my own eyes American citizens quiver like jelly with ecstasy and some embarrassment on meeting a really, truly, honest-to-goodness English lord. Their tongues cleaved to the roof of their mouths as they gurgled and stuttered in the noble presence. We know the silly spectacle that some American women have made of themselves in fishing for an invitation to present their daughters "at court." We know, too, that craven kind of person who when in England seeks to curry favor with the English by scorning and ridiculing his native land and his fellow Americans. Well, I can assure you—if you don't know it already—that our English friends have just as much contempt for that abnormal sort of American as we have. Like us they despise the sycophant who never yet, no matter how long and hard he crawls, has won an honest and wise man's friendship and respect. Like us they have been delighted both in literature and in life to pour scorn on those who would wiggle upward. Do you remember Malvolio in *Twelfth Night* or Uriah Heep in *David Copperfield?* Eternally repeating types.

The trouble is that these would-be Englishmen, these la-dee-da Anglophiles, whom the English don't want as a gift, are likely to irritate a few of us unduly, to distract our attention from the great problems we must meet and to obscure the magnificent qualities of our friends and kinsmen in the rest of the English-speaking world. Let's dismiss them from our thoughts as we would shun their company. They simply don't count in the bigger scheme of things.

The Anglophobe is vicious. He hates England more than he loves America. Racial origin is by no means the usual cause of his abnormality. I have noticed Americans whose ancestors were freedom-loving British men and women who came to our shores two or three centuries ago—Americans who were almost crazed with Anglophobia. Have you never observed the Boston snob (the kind Emerson would have loathed) who fears that despite his educational background he just can't measure up to the cultured English gentleman and therefore relieves his feeling of inferiority by criticizing England with a pathological hatred? The bitterness of an imitation toward the original can be a cruel and dirty thing.

In peaceful times we could dismiss these mentally deformed people with a shrug, regretting that they were afflicted with an ugly obsession just as if they had a harelip. But today we must fight with everything that is in us to keep the Nazi Gestapo out of our lives and the lives of our children—to keep our civilization clean and free. We should be on guard—constantly on guard against these unclean Anglophobes who try to infect us with their own and Hitler's poisons. They pose, of course, as 100 per cent Americans but we must spot them for what they are—enemies of the United States, enemies of our English-speaking civilization, enemies of freedom-loving men and women everywhere whose last great hope rests in the triumph of that civilization. Some of these Anglophobes are so crazed with their hate that they are ineffective. But there are others who are slippery and cunning and who do useful work for their Nazi masters in the form of mental sabotage.

You think this language pretty strong? My fellow countrymen, this war, more than any other in all history, is a struggle for the human mind and the human soul. Hitler has told you that again and again and again. If he and his allies outside and inside America can soften and capture our minds and souls, then our bodies will be ready for the Gestapo's whip.

Yes, let's beware the Anglophobe. Every snarl and whisper of hate against Britain are blows struck at us and our children. They are blows struck in the service of Hitler and his Huns.

How do these Anglophobes work? What are the poisons they try to spread? Why are they a real menace? They dig up stale grudges and invent new lies about our friends and neighbors in our English-speaking world, and with these grudges and lies they trap the decent but uninformed and pander to the mentally unstable people among us. Not many of you have had the time and the energy to dig into the truth which these unscrupulous men conceal or to expose the malicious lies which without the slightest moral restraint they pour out night and day, knowing full well, as Hitler has said, that some of them will stick.

It's pretty hard work to earn a living, to raise a family and to do the duties of an average good citizen. So we have depended on our "intellectuals" to give us the facts and to interpret them as truthfully as they can. Well, some of our "intellectuals" have fought, unwittingly, Hitler's battle and many others simply aren't worth the powder to blow them to Hell—they're too busy screaming at each other and making a pretty penny in the process to speak with the accents of real men—to tell you courageously, soberly, simply what you should know. Perhaps they couldn't tell you if they tried. So many of our self-styled "thinkers" have a lust for self-deception.

I am going to tell you a few things about our fellow democracies in our English-speaking world —things which many of you once knew and may have forgotten or which have not been called to your attention. They are facts all of us should know as we move up to take our place in the battle line of men and women who will still fight and know how to fight for freedom. Some of these facts may give pain to a few of you especially if they step on the toes of old prejudices or ruffle the complacency of entrenched ignorance. But in writing this letter I assume that most of us are now ready, willing, and able to face the truth. It's a good time to brush up our knowledge and clean up our thinking.

Because this is a letter I think it proper at this point to make a confession. I enjoy reading American history more than that of any other nation. To me it's the most interesting. What sweep it has! And power and dash and faith and hope. Above all, what promise—a promise to mankind—a promise which it is our privilege to make good. I suppose being an American has a lot to do with my preference for reading our history. Not entirely of course. I have heard many good citizens, and so must you, who have said that American history was "pretty dull." I think the explanation usually is that they were taught by a weary, cut and dried person who probably spent his days wondering why he hadn't gone into business and earned a fortune rather than "taken up teaching." At any rate, I'm sure that there are many of you who share my enthusiasm for American history and who feel as I do, after making every subtraction, allowance, and concession which Truth and Justice demand, that we can be proud of it and glad to carry on the great tasks it points out for us to do.

And because, in the last analysis, you and I can be proud of our nation's history we can study it fearlessly and learn from our failures and mistakes, see clearly wherein we have sinned and blundered, acknowledge frankly and with grace the help of others, and admit with chastened hearts that in an imperfect world we have had our share of imperfection. That study will give you rich and enduring rewards: the quiet assurance that is bred of true humility and a quickened pride that you, as an American citizen, can play a part, however small, in shaping your country's destiny. We should not forget, especially now, that history is made by many and recorded by few.

When we read the story of our relations with Britain during the last three hundred and thirty-four years, we realize that it has been in great part the story of a family. This land of ours was first settled by Englishmen. Our people have been British subjects for a slightly longer time than they have been American citizens. Nearly all the signers of the Declaration of Independence and the Constitution of the United States were of British ancestry. Our law is based on the English common law. The King James Bible is the Bible most of us read. We talk the same language. I mention these things at this particular point not to emphasize the bonds that unite us in our English-speaking civilization but rather to bring out the reason why certain old grudges, irritations, and untruths have lingered in the minds of some very decent people, a few of whom are today the victims of anti-British propaganda. Family differences are not as easily forgiven and forgotten as those

80

between comparative strangers. Nor are virtues as warmly appreciated and as long remembered. So it has been in our English-speaking family.

Then too, we should remember that for several generations our school histories were written with the obvious purpose of feeding the vanity of a young and self-conscious nation. An honest statement of facts about our past relations with Britain and a fair appraisal of their significance were until recently not only rare but actually attacked by feeble-minded or unscrupulous people as unpatriotic—as if we couldn't look at Uncle Sam, warts and all, and still love him and be willing to die for him. The "cherry tree" myths of history die hard, especially when there is political or financial profit in keeping them alive. And we know that most of us have not read much history since we closed our school books. So the historical distortions and absurdities many people were taught in their early years remained like knots in their minds. In some cases they have been cut out or worn away by wider reading or observation, but the Anglophobe has managed in a few instances to turn those knots into cancerous growths of suspicion and dislike.

You have seen and endured the parlor intellectual who tries to make a conversational impression. When certain examples of Anglo-American co-operation were mentioned, you have heard him say with that asinine air of wisdom which parlor intellectuals have, "Yes, I know—I know—but don't forget that it was to England's interests. Always remember Britain looks after her own interests, ha! ha!" Don't bother to argue with him. Digest your dinner. Turn to the charming lady on your right and enjoy the evening.

Of course it was to England's "interest." And to ours. And to the "interest" of peace and trade and law and order and the stumbling but forward march of democracy throughout our English-speaking civilization. It's to our "interest" to earn a living, to pay taxes, to support the fire and street cleaning departments, the police, the courts, the schools, to crush the forces of brutal might and slavery whenever they threaten us. It's to our "interest" to preserve the blessings of liberty for ourselves and our posterity. It's to Britain's "interest" and to America's "interest" that we cooperate and compete in a free, peaceful, and law-abiding world.

I seem to have dealt quite a bit with rather general considerations, but I think it's a good idea to blow on our glasses and wipe them before reading some facts.

Let's be fair even to George the Third. It's true that he hired German troops to fight us in our revolution. But, under the circumstances, that was a natural thing for him to do. After all, he was more of a German than an Englishman. So many of the British people were on our side that for lack of volunteers to fight us he simply had to turn to the land of his ancestors, the land of the Huns, for the extra troops he needed. (By the way, please remember that it was the ex-Kaiser who first and very proudly named his soldiers Huns.) Moreover, the greatest British statesmen, like Burke and Pitt, vigorously championed our cause in Parliament. Horace Walpole expressed their feelings when in 1777 he wrote to a friend, "I rejoice that the Americans are to be free, as they had a right to be, and as I am sure they have shown they deserve to be. . . . I own there are very able Englishmen left, but they happen to be on t' other side of the Atlantic."

Yes, George the Third was in a bad fix, and he did his German best, but it was not quite good enough. He lacked the necessary support in England. Weak and incompetent as our Congress and politicians were, at least they did not "scuttle and run" like our present crowd. We had decisive help from other nations. We had George Washington, a "country squire," to lead us. And although a Gallup poll might well have shown a majority in favor only of measures "short of war," there were a sufficient number of our ancestors who were "warmongers" and willing to pledge their lives, fortunes, and sacred honor for our freedom.

When our Revolution was won, peace was concluded in the Treaty of Paris of 1783. Benjamin Franklin was the outstanding man of our peace delegation. England sent two negotiators, who were not only old friends of Franklin but also open sympathizers with our Revolution, and one of them, if I remember correctly, had put part of his personal fortune at our disposal during our struggle. Have you forgotten that fact?

The War of 1812 is not one of the glorious pages in American history. Because of it and in the middle of it several New England states almost seceded from the Union. Britain was in a life and death struggle with Napoleon and could devote relatively little effort to the war with us. Even so, we were unable to help autocracy as much as Napoleon had hoped. We were effectively blockaded and rather easily invaded. Our one real land victory—the Battle of New Orleans—took place after the treaty of peace had been signed at Ghent.

Some of you may cherish a grudge because British troops burned the White House in that war. How many of you were told in school or college that American troops had burned the city of Toronto the year before? Two wrongs don't make a right, to be sure, but the first wrong tends to explain although it does not excuse the why and wherefore of the second. The old doctrine of "you

84

hit me first" seems to be rather firmly imbedded in human nature.

Of course you remember that we fought the War of 1812 because England removed people from our ships. It was a genuine grievance. But do you also remember—were you ever taught—that later on we removed people from English ships and that England, although it had a genuine grievance on those occasions, kept her temper and the wrongs we committed were satisfactorily settled by diplomacy in one instance and by arbitration in the other? Some of you were not taught those facts? I wonder why.

The Monroe Doctrine, about which you may have heard, was proposed by the British Prime Minister, George Canning, approved by the Author of the Declaration of Independence, Thomas Jefferson, and announced by the President of the United States, James Monroe. And—incidentally—the British fleet made it stick. The facts about it may seem too obvious to repeat, but in these days when we are urged by men without heart and bowels and liver to flee from the obvious and vital and seek a quivering refuge in the obscure and trivial, it is well to be sure of our A, B, C's. Some intellectuals may moan about "oversimplification." Let 'em moan. It's what they do best.

In 1822 the continent of Europe was in the iron grip of despotism. Four nations—Prussia, Russia, Austria, and France—joined together in what we would today call an "axis" but was then more loftily termed the Holy Alliance. Those nations didn't like England; they didn't like us; and they liked South America very, very much, that is, after a fashion—the way the Nazis do today. Despots in those times were urbane and draped their thoughts gracefully. The first Article of that Alliance said: "The high contracting Powers, being convinced that the system of representative government is as equally incompatible with the monarchical principle as the maxim of sovereignty of the people with the Divine right, engage mutually, in the most solemn manner, to use all their efforts to put an end to the system of representative governments, in whatever country it may exist in Europe, and to prevent its being introduced in those countries where it is not yet known."

The British got the idea. So did we. Appeasers were scarce at the time. What happened was that the Prime Minister put a flea in the ear of Richard Rush, our minister to England. The ultimate danger of the Holy Alliance to us was great. Rush wrote at once to President Monroe, who was no genius but a sensible man not afraid to face obvious facts. He wrote a letter, asking advice, to our greatest living statesman, Thomas Jefferson.

That wise old man was then living in retirement. As you know, he had lived through two wars against England. So he wasn't exactly an Anglophile. And yet twenty-one years before, during his first term as President, he was so clearly aware of Napoleon's threat to our safety that he foresaw the necessity in a pinch to "marry ourselves to the British fleet and nation." The danger of the Holy Alliance was even greater. The wise old man quietly and calmly thought it all over. Much depended on his advice, perhaps the very life of the nation he and Washington and Hamilton and Franklin and Adams and the others had created with so much thought and toil, suffering and sacrifice. It was the gravest question he had considered since those hot July days in Philadelphia nearly a half century before.

I wonder what thoughts went through Thomas Jefferson's mind before he reached for his pen to answer his friend, the President. He might have written that it was fantastic to fear invasion because the ocean was so very, very wide that it took a month to six weeks to cross it. He might have warned against doing anything which would irritate Prussia and her allies. He might have suggested that we start building a super navy which in six or seven years would perhaps be big enough to defend us. He might have sighed and said that, after all, what was the use of trying to oppose the wave of despotism which had swept over the whole European continent, including his beloved

France which he had long before seen and helped achieve liberty, fraternity, and equality. There was only England left. And nine years before, British troops had burned the White House where he had once lived. He might even have repeated the whispers of Fear. "Shut your eyes to the danger— it's not immediate. Wait until America is cornered like a rat. Think of the horrors and agonies of war: the loss of life, the destruction of all those liberties you struggled for, the harm to business."

Yes—Thomas Jefferson might have done any of those things. But he didn't.

On October 23, 1823, the Author of the Declaration of Independence picked up his pen and wrote to Monroe as follows: "The question presented by the letters you have sent me is the most momentous which has ever been offered to my contemplation since that of Independence. That made us a nation, this sets our compass and points the course which we are to steer through the ocean of time opening on us. And never could we embark on it under circumstances more auspicious. . . . One nation, most of all, could disturb us in this pursuit, she now offers to lead, aid, and accompany us in it. By acceding to her proposition, we detach her from the bands, bring her mighty weight into the scale of free government, and emancipate a continent at one stroke, which might otherwise linger long in doubt and difficulty. Great Britain is the nation which can do us the most harm of anyone, or all on earth; and with her on our side we need not fear the whole world. With her then, we should most sedulously cherish a cordial friendship, and nothing would tend more to knit our affections than to be fighting once more, side by side, in the same cause."

Thanks to this unwritten alliance between the British and American navies, America was free for nearly one hundred years from any real menace of invasion. For a century the British fleet preserved a reasonably well-ordered world, and we were thereby able to "mind our own business," prosper, grow great, and cultivate some self-righteous attitudes at little cost or sense of responsibility. So we really didn't become the "greatest nation on earth" all by our very selves. Our most famous naval historian, Admiral Mahan, in his *Influence of Sea Power upon History* honestly recognized that simple fact when he wrote, "Why do English innate political conceptions of popular representative government, of the balance of law and liberty prevail in North America from the Arctic Circle to the Gulf of Mexico, from the Atlantic to the Pacific? Because the command of the sea at the decisive era belonged to Great Britain."

By the way, you can assume as almost certain that not more than one out of twenty Congressmen have ever read Admiral Mahan's book, and it's a good guess that less than ten per cent of them have any real knowledge of American history.

It's true, as you know, that the United States has had several warm disputes, two or three of them quite serious, with Great Britain during the last hundred and twenty-six years. Sometimes we were "in the right" and sometimes "in the wrong." But don't forget they were always settled as warm disputes between reasonable, law-abiding citizens are sensibly settled—by negotiation or arbitration. During our Civil War there were a few such disputes, especially those known as the *"Trent* affair" and the *"Alabama* claims." In the former, England was right, and in the latter America was right.

The *"Trent* affair" arose in 1862 when we removed on the high seas four passengers from the British ship *Trent* and brought them prisoners to Boston—substantially the sort of thing we went to war about in 1812. Our navy captain responsible for the action was hailed as a national hero, wined and dined and eulogized, and even given a vote of thanks by Congress. When the news reached England, there was naturally intense resentment at the outrage. One of Queen Victoria's cabinet ministers even went so far as to prepare an extremely hostile note for her signature. It probably would have meant war. That good and wise woman firmly said, "My lord, you must know that I will agree to no paper that means war with the United

States." A less emphatic protest was sent. We were in the wrong, and Abraham Lincoln was President. So we backed down and made restitution.

England was just as clearly wrong in building cruisers for the Confederacy which sank our merchant ships. The most famous of these cruisers, named the *Alabama,* was built in Liverpool and allowed by the British Government to slip out to sea manned by Confederate officers and sailors. We properly demanded reparation and got it. This time Britain backed down, and as a result of arbitration paid the United States fifteen million dollars in damages.

Much has been written about the sympathetic attitude of the English toward the South. Any honest historian will tell you that England was divided in its opinions about that struggle, just as we were. The English aristocracy sympathized with the aristocratic South, the English liberal and labor classes supported the North so strongly that hundreds of thousands of them actually went hungry rather than help the South to send the cotton upon which their jobs in the mills depended. Because of this "cotton famine" Parliament provided work relief for thousands of cotton operatives in Lancashire (that was seventy years before our Federal Government adopted the "radical" policy of work relief).

This support by the majority of the English

people became even more evident after President Lincoln reversed his position on the slavery question and issued the Emancipation Proclamation. Remember that Lincoln had said in his first inaugural address in March, 1861, that he had no right to interfere with slavery in the South. Here are his words: "Apprehension seems to exist among the people of the Southern States that by the accession of a Republican Administration their property and their peace and personal security are to be endangered. There has never been any reasonable cause for such apprehension. Indeed, the most ample evidence to the contrary ... is found in nearly all the published speeches of him who now addresses you. I do but quote from one of those speeches when I declare that 'I have no purpose, directly or indirectly, to interfere with the institution of slavery in the States where it exists. I believe I have no lawful right to do so, and I have no inclination to do so.' Those who nominated and elected me did so with full knowledge that I had made this and many similar declarations, and had never recanted them."

I suppose that in the light of those words the Emancipation Proclamation might be termed "inconsistent" or even a "broken campaign pledge," and so on, but all of us today think it was not a bad thing. (Have you forgotten that Lincoln did it without asking the permission of Congress and even without consulting the Congressional leaders whose hatred of him grew steadily until his death?)

Remember also that Britain, by peaceful means, without much fuss and feathers, had outlawed slave owning in her colonies a generation before and in her own country more than a half century earlier. Therefore, the moral issue of the Civil War was not clear at first to most Englishmen. Even so, they sensed it from the beginning of that war, and despite all the snubs and pinpricks from her aristocracy and the hardships imposed on her trade by the Northern blockade, England did not recognize the Confederacy as a nation. And, when it comes to pinpricking, we have far outscored our British cousins. At any rate, just as there is no use for Northerners and Southerners to "fight the Civil War all over again," so there is no good reason to keep alive the irritations which then existed between some Englishmen and Americans.

Most of you are probably too young to remember the little Spanish-American War. Certain big European nations, especially Germany, would have welcomed an opportunity to "gang up" on us. Kaiser Wilhelm grimly wrote to a friend after that war, "If I had had a larger fleet I would have taken Uncle Sam by the scruff of the neck." He might have tried it but for John Bull. While Admiral Dewey was stationed at Manila Bay, shortly after his victory, a German naval squadron, stronger than Dewey's, appeared on the scene. Also present was a strong British squadron. "What would you do," the German admiral asked the English admiral, "in the event of trouble between Admiral Dewey and myself?" The Englishman coolly replied, "That is a secret known only to Admiral Dewey and me." The German returned to his flagship, and the next morning he saw a British cruiser stationed between Dewey and himself. It was the kind of language Germans understand, and he sailed away. I think the ghosts of George Canning and Thomas Jefferson and James Monroe must have winked at each other and smiled with grim satisfaction as they remembered the job they did back in 1823.

My fellow countrymen, I haven't the time or space in this letter to give you in great detail the history of Anglo-American relations. I am simply calling your attention to some of the big and important facts—facts which the pro-Nazi and anti-British propagandists among our pseudo intellectuals and cheapjohn politicians, our reactionaries and our Communists have suppressed or twisted or distorted for their evil purposes. And so, I have not mentioned several other examples of friendly co-operation or unhappy differences. There have been, as you know, a few disputes and trivial squabbles about boundaries and canal tolls and

fisheries. But never lose sight of the big thing—
that Britain and America have lived, competed,
and co-operated in peace with each other and
have always settled their differences in a reasonable and law-abiding manner.

BRITAIN AND AMERICA:
ALIKE AND UNLIKE

This is a good time, late as it is, to see in what ways we—British and Americans—are alike and unlike.

Britain is, of course, in some ways more democratic and more progressive than the United States. Yes, brothers and sisters, it's a fact—one of those plain, simple facts which madden the Anglophobes and which even the honest element among our intellectuals is scared to admit publicly. I'll tell you in a moment why and in what ways Britain is more democratic and progressive than we are.

Now then, I don't mean that there are more opportunities to make money in England. There aren't. Nature alone gives us more opportunity—that little island in the North Sea is less than one third the size of Texas. We have actually and relatively many more millionaires. I don't mean that the British produce or own as many newfangled gadgets and automobiles and refrigerators and cosmetics and plumbing facilities. They don't. In money and mechanics we're tops. Which is fine and nothing to be ashamed about. We can take honest pride in the material development of America even after making proper allowance for the crimes and blunders, the knavish dishonesties and sickening brutalities committed in the process of "conquering a continent." But next year's model automobile doesn't mean more "democracy" and it means "progress" only in a very narrow material sense. Surely we Americans don't think that progress is solely or almost entirely material—if so, our only boast would be that America is the biggest, best, most streamlined and up-to-date human pigsty on earth. And, assuming that we must boast to remain somewhat sure of ourselves, we wouldn't want that to be our loudest or only boast. Well—most of us wouldn't.

Another thing. If you are one of those hot-eyed people who believe that existing democracy is a fake and that we are all the helpless tools of dishonest rich men, there isn't much use reading on. That has been for several years a money-making theme of certain notorious writers. Sometimes I think more money has been gained by writing about how our rich men got money dishonestly than our rich men dishonestly got.

You and I know that democracy in both countries is imperfect, and our imperfections make some of our intellectuals, who are not exactly perfect, nervously impatient—which strikes me as a

97

bit ungrateful because they thrive and prosper and grow fat on our imperfection. At any rate, we know, without their chattering and gibbering, that democracy throughout our English-speaking world has often faltered and stumbled, failed and blundered, but that somehow it keeps marching forward. Because we English-speaking peoples want freedom more than life itself and because we are a bit suspicious of perfection in this world, our democratic ideals have made a slow, rough, and, at times, heartbreaking advance. My point is, that in judging democracy, past and present, in Britain and America, we must always keep an eye on the "end figure" and we shall see that it is plus and not minus in the life of mankind.

Now, then, in what ways is Britain more democratic than we are? Well—in its government. The supreme governmental power in Great Britain is the House of Commons, elected by the people. The Prime Minister cannot veto an act of Parliament. Of course the King cannot. There is no Supreme Court which can declare legislation unconstitutional. The veto power of the House of Lords (like our Senate, the "upper chamber") was taken away more than thirty years ago. The Prime Minister has not a fixed term like that of our President. He cannot stay in office for a definite period whether or not a majority of the people's representatives in the Commons want him to stay.

When they say "no confidence" he's out—unless he appeals directly to the people and a majority of them say "You're not doing a bad job—we're still for you."

In the United States governmental power is equally distributed among the executive, legislative, and judicial branches which "check and balance" one another. Congress and the people may think that the President is doing a bad job, but they can't remove him as the House of Commons and the British people can remove their chief executive. Mind you, the British system, by and large, has worked well for the British people and our system, by and large, has worked well for us. I'm not saying that their system is better but simply that it is more democratic than ours. Would you like to see our House of Representatives have the same power in this country as the House of Commons has in England? You wouldn't? I wonder why.

"All right," some of you will say, "but in this country a man may be born in a log cabin and regardless of his race or creed he can become President." Quite true. Well—wait a minute. Partly true. Most of our presidents and, with the exception of Lincoln, certainly the greatest of them were born in wealthy or at least comfortable circumstances. (Despite all our romanticizing and gushing about the dear, old log cabins and their rustic democracy they have not yet become "all the rage" for our own living purposes.) Let's admit, however, that a poor boy can become President. "Regardless of race or creed"? Not yet. Has a Jew become President? Not yet. Or Chief Justice of the Supreme Court? Not yet. Or Secretary of State? Not yet. Do you remember the presidential campaign of 1928? Have we ever elected a labor leader to the presidency?

We know that one of England's greatest Prime Ministers, Benjamin Disraeli, was a Jew, that the radical son of a humble Scotch farm girl and that a poor, obscure Welsh lawyer became Prime Ministers, that an iron molder who was a manual laborer until twenty-nine years old achieved fame as a Secretary for Foreign Affairs, that a poor Jewish lad became Lord Chief Justice of England and later Viceroy of India, a land he first saw as a cabin boy, and that today labor is a full partner in the British Government. Do you know, it's possible that we may learn a lot more about democracy from our friends and kinsmen in England.

But Britain has an aristocracy. Yes. And we have a plutocracy. In the British aristocracy are many men who place their country's welfare above their own interest and a few rich men who don't, and in our plutocracy are a few men with a sense of responsibility to others (the hallmark of aristocracy) who place their country's welfare above their wealth and too many who don't. Our aristocracy, both Southern and Northern, died at Appomattox in 1865. Our plutocrats of the Newport and Palm Beach variety, who spend loads of money pretending to be what they aren't, merely ape the superficial aspects of the fast-disappearing British aristocracy but not its magnificent qualities of honor and duty and self-sacrifice which the English people have appreciated in the past and again today have called upon from Winston Churchill. As for the so-called night club "smart set" in London and New York—they attract about the same amount of attention and pull about the same weight in both countries as the characters in our "funny papers."

Of course, there are many examples in both Britain and America of men who have risen from humble circumstances to positions of eminence in the professions, in politics and in business by virtue of their character, energy, ability, and good luck. Their distinction and their public service are sometimes rewarded in England with a nice title and in this country with a long obituary. Let's not begrudge them either.

If we wished, we could spend days and nights pointing out wherein democracy has not yet fully succeeded in Britain and the British could do the same about our lack of success. You know what I mean. There are miserable slums in the East End of London—and equally miserable slums on the East Side and in the Harlem section of New York City; conditions are bad among the coal miners in Wales—and equally so among the coal miners in Kentucky; the poorer English farm tenants lack adequate plumbing in their houses—and our share-croppers lack adequate food in their stomachs; college education is not as widespread in England —and graft and corruption are far more widespread here; too many British politicians were educated at Eton and Oxford—and too many American politicians obviously have never been educated at all. Yes, we could carry on a long, long time picking out and bewailing the unpleasant shortcomings and tragic mistakes of both peoples. That is a peacetime luxury. We have a matter of life and death to decide now.

We are more alike than unlike. That is why we shall soon be comrades-in-arms in this war and full-fledged partners in the peace to come. But we must be mature enough to realize that there are also strength and richness and mutual benefit in our unlikenesses. The men and women of Alabama and Vermont, of Massachusetts and Mississippi, of Rhode Island and Oklahoma are somewhat unlike yet American. And Americans, Australians, Canadians, Englishmen, New Zealanders, and South Africans are somewhat unlike yet members and neighbors of the English-speaking family. Behind each and every one of us in that family are the blood, tears, toil, and sweat of a thousand years. Government with the consent of the governed, freedom of the individual under the law which he has helped to make, individual opportunity with proper regard for the rights of one's neighbors, protection for the helpless and the unfortunate—these are the things we English-speaking peoples have lived for, killed for, and will die for. We just can't help it—we've been made that way, through a thousand years. And we'll go on that way.

Let's take another look backward for a moment. It will help make clear that our present struggle to live as free men is not only supremely worth while but perfectly natural. I have time and space in this letter to recall only a few things which have made us English-speaking peoples what we are.

Some of our shyster historians and unclean Anglophobes may have given a few of you the impression that representative government, personal liberty, and modern social reforms were American inventions which the rest of the English-speaking nations, especially Britain, slowly and reluctantly imitated. It's the other way around. Those things were born in England and grew there long before they were spread by Englishmen to other parts of the world, including Jamestown and Plymouth, or taken over by us and applied to our own needs.

103

They have had a slow, rough growth here as in Britain, and they are still in the process of perfection and will be as long as our civilization survives. When we have become a community of saints (which I think a merciful God will not permit on earth), then the process will stop.

Long before the Norman conquest, the Anglo-Saxons began their experiment with representative government in their "witenagemot," a group of men elected to legislate for the needs and desires of their locality. In the thirteenth century the first national parliament met and made laws, and during the next two hundred years the members of Parliament were busy passing laws of all kinds including many to fix prices, restrain unfair trade practices, and otherwise regulate business. The Tudor monarchs were a high-handed lot, and Parliament usually did their bidding, but even Queen Elizabeth, in the sixteenth century, had a healthy regard for the Commons and wisely realized that her power was not absolute. Charles the First in the seventeenth century was not so wise and lost his head after a grim civil war won by the plain people—the Puritans—of England under the leadership of men like Cromwell and Hampden, Pym and Milton. In the eighteenth century the responsibility of the Prime Minister and his cabinet to the House of Commons was finally established. Meanwhile the English settlers in this country, during the seventeenth and eighteenth centuries, had established their legislative bodies such as the Virginia House of Burgesses and the Massachusetts General Court. The majority of men both in America and in Britain at the time of our Revolution did not have the absolute right to vote. There were property qualifications in both countries. And at that time the British Parliament, with some magnificent exceptions, was almost as venal, corrupt, and incompetent as our Congress was after the Civil War—about a hundred years later. The people in both countries would not be denied. There are now no requirements of property ownership in either country for the right to vote, although in some sections of the United States, both North and South, certain poll taxes still prevent the very poor from voting. Britain, as we have seen, became even more democratic by taking away the veto power of the House of Lords whereas our Senate has become in practice more powerful than the House of Representatives. Finally in this twentieth century the vote was given to the ladies in both countries on their frantic assurance that our politics would be thereby raised to the very gates of heaven.

Most of the "Fathers of the Republic" read and thought and felt deeply. They knew history and were thoroughly versed in the political philosophy of the great Englishmen like Coke, Bolingbroke,

Locke, Hampden, Vane, and Milton. (The most magnificent defense of freedom of the press in our language is Milton's *Areopagitica*—read it if you truly wish to understand much of our English-speaking civilization, past and present.) The "Fathers" were steeped in the British tradition of parliamentary government; and, when the hour of decision struck, they had in Oliver Cromwell a mighty precedent for the last resort of revolution by force. When our political independence was achieved, they did not slavishly imitate the British form of government but wisely applied the English political philosophy to our own needs and circumstances. They also built much that was new in government but they built on the bedrock of their Anglo-Saxon past.

Most of those wise and learned men were thoroughly grounded in the English common law, which is our law as well as England's. They knew what many Americans today tragically fail to realize—that the supremacy of the law is the surest safeguard of the liberties of the people. Long before their time the battle against arbitrary power had been led by the greatest master of the common law, Sir Edward Coke. In November, 1608, there took place between him and King James the First one of the most important personal interviews in modern history. Coke firmly explained to that arbitrary sovereign what the common law meant. Said Coke: "The king in his own person cannot adjudge any case either criminal . . . or betwixt party and party." Moreover, "The king cannot take any cause out of any of his courts and give judgment upon it himself." His Majesty angrily retorted, "This means that I shall be under the law which it is treason to affirm." "To which," writes Coke, "I replied that Bracton saith, *quod Rex non debet esse sub homine, sed sub Deo et lege.*" (Translated for those who, like myself, have forgotten what little Latin they ever knew: "Because the king ought not to be under man, but under God and the law.")

Personal liberty—freedom of speech, freedom of worship, freedom of the press, freedom from unlawful search and seizure—all those things without which life is not worth living for us English-speaking men and women—they were made in England. To be sure they have been momentarily in danger and even wickedly violated there and here, and certain it is that we must always be vigilant to protect and eager to strengthen them. I think we care about them a good deal. They are in our Bill of Rights. We have long taken them for granted as we do the air we breathe. Yes, I think most of us care about them as much as the British do. We're alike, you see, in the things that count. Not only because we want to be but simply because we can't help it. That's why we shall "be fighting once more, side by side, in the same cause."

Perhaps the most vital aspect of our English-speaking civilization is its emphasis on the individual man (you and me)—his safety from physical abuse or theft or tyranny by his fellows or by his government, his self-respect and integrity as a member of society, his very real importance as a human being, his spirit and conscience as one of the children of God whether or not he believes in Him. Trial by jury, habeas corpus, the rules of evidence, the laws of property and wills and inheritance, the relief of equity—these are some of the safeguards of civilization which in one way or another affect each one of us. They are the products of no intellectual's blueprint for a perfect society or of a tyrant's scheme for a "new order" but of trial and error, of many wise men's judgments, brave men's fights, and plain men's daily experience—products which were English in their origins and in the development of which both Britain and America have shared. The struggle for your and my right to worship as we please and deem fitting—or not to worship at all—is one of the saddest, cruelest, and yet most triumphant in the record.

In Britain that protection and respect for each man's mind and personality and body and property are even more highly developed than in the

United States. That is one reason why an Englishman's love of "privacy" is at times misunderstood and mistakenly ascribed by some of us to snobbishness. Many Americans have too much reverence for a majority and too little respect for the minority—and yet democracy means, among other things, a proper balance between that reverence and that respect. But, in the last analysis, all of us men and women—Americans and British—are alike in needing these personal freedoms and their safeguards, as we need light and air and sunshine, simply to live. During the last ten centuries we English-speaking peoples, in our struggle for liberty, have ground in the dust thousands of tyrants and their evil accomplices. Hitler's attack on our liberty is of course an outrage—but we must prove to mankind that it is also an impertinence.

The so-called "social reforms" of recent times were introduced in Britain earlier than in the United States. That was natural because the need for them there became more apparent and more urgent much earlier than here. Her Industrial Revolution began about fifty years before ours. (Like it or not, these "reforms" have only started because they are simply adjustments which human society must make from time to time, and there's plenty of adjusting ahead of us.) The abolition of slavery, as we have seen, was peacefully achieved in England long before we did it by civil war. Unemployment relief was first and successfully tried in Lancashire in 1863, under an act of Parliament, and later, on a national scale, after the last war. Such "socialistic" measures as unemployment insurance and employment bureaus were proposed more than thirty years ago by radicals like David Lloyd George and Winston Churchill and were adopted by Parliament. The English have done a far bigger job than we have in slum clearance and housing projects for the underprivileged. Our government has publicly acknowledged the splendid pioneering work already done in Britain. At any rate, we—Americans and British—have had more or less similar problems of social and economic adjustment, and we've been alike in dealing with them in a democratic and experimental sort of way, making mistakes while making progress.

It should be especially noted by some of you that the British Conservative Party is proud of its achievements in these respects and has striven to outdo its Labour Party opponents. Just as our "liberals" can learn—and to a certain extent have learned—much from English liberalism, so our "conservatives" can learn—but unfortunately have not learned—a good deal by studying the Conservative Party's record. It was a long time ago—seventy years or more—that a wise Tory genially remarked that he "caught the Whigs in bathing and stole their clothes."

It's true that in trying to pay off the terrific costs of the last war and in spending vast sums for the social betterment of the people the British failed to prepare against the growing menace of Hitlerism. But let's remember that disarmament during the prewar years was the favorite lullaby of "liberals" and indeed of most people throughout the English-speaking democracies. It wasn't until last June that our Congress woke up with a jump. England wasn't "ready for war." Neither are we. And we never have been prepared for war. That's part of the steep price we pay for democracy. But, though unready, we have fought to become an independent and to remain a united people. Now we shall fight to save our national existence and the only kind of world in which we can live as a free democracy.

Very few Americans know what the British Empire is. And very few Englishmen do. But it's worth while to note a few general facts about it so that we can better combat the anti-British propaganda of the Nazis and their friends in this country.

As you know, there have been three great periods in the development of the Empire—the colonial, the autonomous, and the present partnership, called the British Commonwealth of Na-

111

tions. They all overlap somewhat, but that has been the general trend. Remember that the British Empire is a world power and that all parts of the world don't move at the same time, in the same direction, and at the same speed. Our self-styled "thinkers" with their psychopathic terror of plain, obvious facts try to forget that when they sob today about India or some of the African colonies. But the trend throughout the Empire has been steadily toward political liberty and independent partnership of the peoples within it. Today, the British Commonwealth is such a partnership of nations including Great Britain, Canada, Australia, New Zealand, and South Africa. These nations are free and equal; they manage their own internal affairs; appoint their own diplomatic representatives; make their own treaties; can remain at peace or declare war as they see fit and can secede from the Empire any time they choose. And yet the Empire is stronger today than ever before. The Nazi mind couldn't possibly understand why. We Americans can grasp the idea because we are a member, the greatest single member, of the English-speaking family. The biggest reason is that these nations in the Commonwealth are free. Another is that the Empire represents the kind of political society they want—an Anglo-Saxon civilization in which political and personal liberty is as matter-of-fact as bread and water. (It includes Dutch and

French-Canadian minorities but they are content because they live in freedom.) Then too, there is the mystic and deeply personal loyalty to the Crown. That is one of those mighty intangibles which cannot be defined or successfully analyzed. Like the religious instinct in most of us it cannot be measured or weighed. But it is supremely real. Our reverence for the Flag is the closest analogy I can think of. How can we account for that inner surge of joy, the quickened heart beat, the flashing consciousness of a fierce loyalty when we see Old Glory passing by—even more so when we are away from the homeland? Well—there are some things we understand without words.

Yes—the trend of Anglo-American civilization is toward more liberty, more democracy, more life. Nazism means death. My guess is that our civilization will live.

Does someone want a catalogue of the crimes and blunders that we have committed in building that civilization? I haven't the space—it would be a voluminous thing. I leave that task to the scrupulous historian, the sensitive poet, the observing dramatist, the honest public servant, the learned judge, the alert journalist, the plain man and woman. Those crimes and blunders are a cause for shame and reformation; they are a challenge to do right as it is given us to see the right; they should not lead us into the moral suicide which

113

some of our exhibitionist intellectuals are messily committing. We know—we English-speaking men and women know that our direction is right and that, united, we are strong enough to go ahead.

I want to say a few words about our closest neighbor and most understanding friend in our Anglo-American family—I mean that great nation to the north of us—Canada. It's unfortunate but not surprising that most Americans do not know very much about Canada. New Yorkers, for example, are generally quite "provincial" in their knowledge of what lies west of the Hudson river, and I'm sure that many Bostonians still think it's the intellectual boundary line of American civilization. Then, too, our Canadian friends have not devoted their talents and energies to advertising on a really big scale their virtues and achievements. They seem to be rather quaintly content to do the job at hand, do it well and not talk much about it. The strong Scottish strain in them may account for this slightly old-fashioned way of doing things. Mind you, they are immensely hospitable, as many of us know, and they'll listen with flattering and genuine interest while we tell them about our hard problems and great deeds. We could learn a lot if we listened as much to them.

Moreover, a great many Canadians have had American ancestors and a large number of Americans have had Canadian parents. There has been from colonial times a big flow of people back and forth across our boundary lines. Some of our finest professional and businessmen are Canadian-born, and American-born men have contributed splendidly to Canada's greatness. Incidentally, for some time she has been our best customer in the whole world. The Canadian government is more flexible and, like the British, more directly responsive to the people, but in their fundamental political and social ideals the Canadians and Americans are alike. Of course, the United States and Canada have had disputes, as good neighbors do—mostly about fish and real estate—but they've been ironed out, and no grudges have remained. In short, we like and trust each other.

But Canada is a great nation in her own right. She's proud of being next to the oldest partner in the British Commonwealth of Nations. And her loyalty to Britain is no mere lip service. Her faith in Anglo-Saxon civilization, in democracy, in personal freedom does not stop short of—paying the price for them. Canada is the British Empire's best witness. She was free to do as she liked when this war broke out. She did so—as she had done before in 1914—she stood with Britain in the ranks of freedom. And don't forget that her casualties in the last war were nearly equal to as well as relatively greater than ours although we have twelve times her population. Again today, Canada is in the battle line with her men in an expeditionary force, on the seas, and in the air, and giving half her income directly to the cause. And she's happy. Which we soon shall be when we really start doing the job that must be done.

We do not yet appreciate—and the Canadians themselves are probably too busy to realize—what an effective and decisive part Canada is playing in this war. I am referring not only to her military efforts which are becoming more obvious and more splendid day by day. There is something even more important than that for us and our children. Canada has become, as never before, the mighty bridge of a better understanding and a warmer sense of kinship between the British Empire and the United States. She is bridging the gap which certain superficial differences have created between Englishmen and Americans. Yes, superficial indeed, as we now know, but sufficient in times past to cause needless irritations and absurd suspicions. It is given to Canada to help bring about the mightiest and most enduring friendship in the history of nations. If she can do that, it will be the noblest achievement of any country in modern times. Did I say "if"? She is doing it by word and deed, by her superb and unquenchable loyalty to Britain and by her daily acts of friendship to America.

If ever a nation deserved loyalty, it is Britain

now. She has won such a loyalty as she has never had before—loyalty from her sons and daughters throughout the Empire, from her kinsmen and friends in America, from people throughout the world who want to remain or pray to become free. They know that if Britain lives freedom lives.

The British people once again are the pioneers of human liberty. The Mother Country of the English-speaking nations is leading the way to a better world. It is our privilege to be in her company, to share her burden, and with her to fight the good fight.

Yes, I said "privilege" and I mean it. Because the men and women of Britain have made us no longer ashamed of the eternal values, the supreme human virtues. For a while men desperately tried to find cheap and sordid and coldly selfish reasons for their own and others' actions. The doctrine of "self-interest," the philosophy and ethical standards of the hogpen were supposed to guide us in all we thought and did. We winced under the Nazi and Communist jibes at our old faith and basic ideals.

The English have given them back to us. They have poured life and meaning into our greatest words and have restored them to their ancient primacy in our language and in our hearts. Words like Truth, Justice, Freedom, Mercy and Humility, Faith and Fortitude, Prayer and Sacrifice, Love

117

and Duty. We know again what they mean—thanks to England. Out of their blood, tears, toil, and sweat the men and women and children of Britain have made a heroic age and have restored to the world the only things for which free peoples will fight and die. Their sacrifices will spare us much of their suffering, but at least we Americans must give all that lies in our power. That is our duty and our privilege.

We in America can never quite repay our debt to the British people in this war. And that is not only because they are hurling back the Nazi barbarians day and night while we get ready. More than that. They have taught us again that democracy can be tough; that democracy can summon from its people a supreme devotion more lasting than a ruthless fanaticism begotten of cruelty and lies; that democracy can make a better world than any system, however efficient, which buys so-called "material progress" at the price of the Gestapo and the degradation of the human spirit. They have taught us that we are fighting a classless war, a war of the plain people, a war of the little homes, a war for those simple decencies without which life is not worth living. And they have taught us in America that the English and Scotch and Welsh peoples today are not our ancestors but our contemporaries, our neighbors, our friends, the same kind of men and women as we are.

And their magnificent leader, Winston Churchill, is the living symbol of the underlying unity of the English-speaking world, a unity which is the best hope for the future of mankind. A heroic people and a heroic age need a heroic leader. Such is Churchill. When America has hit her stride, when she has taken her rightful place on the battle line of freedom, then we Americans shall be entitled to take pride that Winston Churchill is the worthy product of an Anglo-American alliance, that he is our man as well as England's.

Some people, especially the younger generation who have been so thoroughly educated in the hog-pen theories of modern thought, are amazed in a manner reminiscent of Paul of Tarsus on the road to Damascus, by the revelation of the British spirit. They need not be. It is an old story—older than the United States.

More than half a century before the first English settlers came to Jamestown and Plymouth the great churchman, Bishop Latimer, was burned at the stake for his religious beliefs. Just as the fires were lighted, he turned to his friend at the stake next to him and said: "Play the man, Master Ridley; we shall this day light such a candle, by God's grace, in England, as I trust shall never be put out."

That, my friends, is why there'll always be an England.

BRITAIN AND AMERICA:
THEY WILL DO THE JOB

Uncle Sam has made much progress, since September, 1939, along the dark and rough road toward the peace and freedom of mankind. He has wallowed in the Slough of Despond; was held prisoner in the dungeon of Giant Despair; been tempted by the glittering goods and wares of Vanity Fair; momentarily deceived by Mr. Facing-both-ways. He still has ahead of him a terrific fight with the Nazi Apollyon. But he will not be alone. Mr. Greatheart of the British Empire will be fighting with him. Even when they reach their great destination together and enjoy the peace and freedom for which they have fought and suffered —even then they must work hard and gladly to keep what they have won.

During these last hours before America marches into battle we must be on guard against the tricks and wiles of Hitler and his isolationist allies who will stop at nothing to keep us "at peace" or at least "short of war." You and I are hearing and reading a good deal these days about "unity" and "tolerance." Those are fine things which we want and should strive to have. But be on guard. Those good words are being used by men of evil intentions to check and weaken our efforts to destroy Hitler and all his works. Our notorious appeasers and isolationists talk sweetly about the "need for unity" before we do anything. They plead and whine for "tolerance" and against "name calling." Tolerance toward whom and what? Themselves, who daily do Hitler's will and preach, in large part knowingly, the doctrines of moral cowardice and national suicide? "Tolerance" toward slavery and torture, toward black-hearted men and their willing or obedient followers, toward the vile and crafty forces which threaten to mangle and crush the common decencies and precious liberties of our lives and our children's lives? "Tolerance" toward conscious or unconscious betrayal? "Tolerance" toward those vicious men who whine for a peace without freedom—a "negotiated" peace— the peace of death?

And "unity." What do these false appeasers, these deathly isolationists, these tricksters of Hitler—what do they mean? Unity with whom and for what? "Unity" with them? "Unity" for their and Hitler's purposes? "Unity" with fear and delay? "Unity" with Nazism and ruin?

No. We won't be fooled any longer by those tricks. Most Americans now are wise to them. We have come to ourselves. We are once more masters of our own destiny as a free people—not nervously waiting for Hitler and his allies to determine our policy. And that means—Hitler must go. The voice of America has grown clear and firm and it is saying to the Führer:

"You have preached pure evil for many years and you have the solitary merit of practicing what you preach. You have debased the mind and corrupted the hearts of the German people—especially the young, whom you have crazed with the lusts of cruelty and power; you have tortured and driven into exile men and women of the Jewish race, partly no doubt because of your maddening sense of inferiority to them and partly because your evil genius told you that a sure way to the dark chambers of the soul of man is the path of intolerance; you turned the German nation into the mightiest and most efficient criminal force in all history, and decent men, free men, honest men, kind men in your own land and everywhere on earth feared and despised you. And yet, Herr Hitler, you will lose.

"You conquered two nations with your lies and then, when your other peace-loving neighbors began to face the facts, you struck them down while they groped too late and in vain amidst treachery and confusion for the means to ward off and to return the blow. For the moment they are in your power. Austria, Czechoslovakia, Poland, Denmark,

Norway, Luxembourg, Holland, Belgium, France, Yugoslavia, Greece. They are in your power. But, according to the clock of history, only for a moment. Two or three years, perhaps. Because, Herr Hitler, you will lose.

"You have caused much suffering and destroyed much beauty in the Mother Country of the English-speaking nations. Your bombers have carefully maimed and killed old men and women and children, the innocent and the helpless. They have marred or ruined venerable churches, great buildings, and ancient landmarks which for centuries have been the physical evidence of the spiritual things we cherish most. And you will cause more suffering and do more damage to our friends and kinsmen across the sea. Even so, Herr Hitler, you will lose.

"You tried to kill the spirit of America. You wanted to take from us our moral manhood so that we would feel a cold indifference toward right and wrong. For a little while, here and there, you were horribly successful, partly because you enlisted some kindred spirits among us, some pseudo economists and shyster historians, some scheming Communists and gullible businessmen, and, most pathetic of all, some honest, well-meaning folk who seemed to think, as did good folk five centuries ago, that the earth is flat and that

123

the world ends at the ocean's horizon. You appealed to our Pontius Pilates who told us to wash our hands of the 'mess.' Your agents sobbed about the 'Crime of Versailles' while you bombed and enslaved nation after nation. Some of our whining intellectuals pleaded, like you, for 'justice' toward your 'rightful claims' while thousands of honest, free-thinking men and women writhed in the torture of your concentration camps. You have left no stone unturned, no trick untried to confuse our minds and to harden our hearts. And even at this eleventh hour you are still trying—ingeniously, desperately trying to kill the American spirit. But, Herr Hitler, you will lose."

There are, of course, many kindly people who are disturbed by the thought that in our midst are men of ill will and with evil designs against our democratic ideals and our Anglo-American civilization. It may comfort these worthy people to realize that unanimity has seldom if ever been achieved in man's long journey from the jungle. It is one of the silly trade-marks of the perfectionists. Progress has been made by various groups of people despite blind opposition and black treachery within their ranks. The degree of opposition and treachery has varied and is not predictable. In a quite well-known group, two thousand years ago, it was one in twelve. In our Revolutionary War the proportion was much greater, and it's a debatable question whether, if a poll had been taken in 1775, a majority of Americans would have voted for war—the vote might have been only for measures "short of war." If you're interested enough to dig into the history of that time, you'll find that some of our "best people" in New York and Philadelphia greeted the British officers with feasting and good cheer; that many plain people did not lift a finger to help the American cause; that the farmers near Valley Forge did not give anything from their well-stocked barns to the hungry men fighting their battle; that men were bribed a thousand dollars or more apiece to fight under Washington and they often took the bribe and ran away; that the colonies did not fill one-sixth of their quotas for troops; that there were weak and unscrupulous men in Congress then as now. Our Constitution was adopted only by a narrow squeak. The states were fearful of surrendering some of their sovereignty for the common good—it took Alexander Hamilton's supreme efforts to bring New York into the Union. As for the Civil War—well, it wasn't all "Abe" Lincoln and Battle Hymns and the "boys in blue." Have you forgotten about the "draft riots," which were partly race riots, in Northern cities? Did you know that well-to-do citizens in the North hired substitutes to serve for them in the Union armies and that in many cases men auctioned their services to the highest bidder—the price sometimes reaching fifteen hundred dollars? Do you remember reading about the conscienceless profiteering which was in great part the foundation of our plutocracy? Have you read about the contempt, hatred, and treachery which Lincoln suffered but overcame in his own ranks? It turned out all right in the Revolution, in the state conventions adopting the Constitution, and in the Civil War. There were a sufficient number of true Americans to win in every case. But there wasn't "unity." And there was no treacherous "tolerance" shown to the enemies within our ranks.

One of the last-minute appeals to fear and self-deception is familiar to most of you. It is that the United States of America will become a permanent dictatorship—"go totalitarian"—take away our liberties forever if it goes to war. A few good people are innocently and several bad people are purposely repeating that ancient lie. Naturally, when we go to war we shall give up for its duration many of the rights, privileges, luxuries, and pleasures of peacetime. And of course that's one of the big reasons why the decent, peace-loving, law-abiding men and women in our English-speaking democracies hate war. But it's either silly or malicious to argue that when free men band together and submit to essential discipline so that they may crush the tyranny which threatens them

126

and their homes they destroy their own freedom. It's true that we can't fight gangsters who are roaming about our neighborhood and be as blithe and free as when they don't trouble us. We can't fight a fire which menaces our homes and go to the movies at the same moment. We can choose, of course, which to do. Wars are rough and ugly and tragic, but we could no more surrender or permit anyone to take away our liberties permanently than we could jump over the moon. We English-speaking peoples are simply made that way. That's what Hitler and some of our whining intellectuals cannot quite understand. Which is perfectly natural, because they are made very, very differently.

Have you forgotten that, during the Civil War, Lincoln suspended the writ of habeas corpus so that the Government could and did arrest and imprison people on mere suspicion without trial? Do you remember what the Great Emancipator said in 1863 about the effect of wartime measures on our civil liberties? Read again his words, consult your common sense, and your hearts will not be troubled. "I am unable," said Honest Abe, "to appreciate the danger apprehended that the American people will, by means of military arrests during the Rebellion, lose the right of public discussion, the liberty of speech and the press, the laws of evidence, trial by jury, and habeas corpus, throughout the indefinite peaceful future which I trust lies before them, any more than I am able to believe that a man could contract so strong an appetite for emetics during a temporary illness as to persist in feeding upon them during the remainder of his healthful life." I think most of us share Lincoln's faith in the living traditions and good sense of our democracy.

There's a lot of talk these days about "war aims" and "peace aims." Some of it is being done, of course, by our pro-Nazi and anti-British propagandists for sabotage purposes, but I won't discuss those vicious people any more in this letter. I've paid my respects to them. A good deal of this talk is being done by honest, able, high-minded men and women. Many of them appreciate Winston Churchill's remark to the effect that if Britain stopped fighting we would soon find out what the fighting was about. But it seems to me that some of these splendid citizens have overlooked one or two practical little items which require our immediate attention. We have a war to win—Hitler to beat—before we can make a world nearer to our heart's desire. We must earn our reward before we wisely enjoy it. In other words, we must contribute our full share of the "blood, toil, tears, and sweat" needed for a common victory. If we don't, our talk and advice won't amount to a damn in building and maintaining a better world. America cannot get self-respect and the respect of others "on the cheap."

But we shall do our share. On that basis it will be wise and helpful for us to do some hard thinking about what lies ahead. It's too early, and there are too many uncertain factors for us to adopt any definite blueprint for the future. However, we can and must face certain big facts without flinching—if the best part of our civilization is to live and grow. I'll jot down a few of them.

We must avoid treacherous sentimentality in the peace terms. That sentimentality was largely responsible for the unchecked growth and early successes of the Nazi power. I've pointed that out before, but I do it again because it's so awfully important. Our sentimentalists have blood on their hands—not their blood. If we are again deceived by the German whine in defeat, by our slushy self-styled "thinkers," by well-meaning people of the "forgive and forget" school, then we'll have Germany again grabbing at our throats in another twenty-five years.

The world has suffered enough within the memory of people still living from the brute militarism of Germany which has grown more and more bestial as it developed under Chancellor Bismarck, Kaiser Wilhelm, and Herr Hitler. When the English-speaking democracies have won this war, they must leave no doubt of their victory in the minds and memories of the German people and no chance for "stab in the back" legends to revive their lust for power over others. We must remember that in Germany after this war there will be millions of the younger generation whose minds have been permanently warped by the Nazi teachings and in whose sullen hearts will be smoldering the lusts of cruelty and power. It will take more than a well-meaning intellectual or a beaming Y.M.C.A. secretary to deal with them. I don't know what the solution is, but we simply must find and face it no matter how stern it may be and despite all the shrieks and sobs of our sentimentalists who will again help to wreck the peace of the world if given a chance.

Another big fact. Either isolationism as a national policy must die or our sons will. Of course all the isolationists won't die—there'll be several of them in our midst just as there are still people who think the world is flat, and both should be treated alike. The isolationists, as well as the sentimentalists, are blood-stained men and women. The sincerity of some of them merely adds to the vast human tragedy for which they are largely responsible. They have helped Hitler enough. And along with isolationism must go the cowardly and dishonest policy of "moral support." It is neither truly moral nor real support, and is satisfying only to those drunk with self-righteousness.

The United States and the British Commonwealth will be partners in the peace they both must win. That's a big fact we can gladly face. We —the English-speaking democracies—must do as partners what Britain did alone for more than a hundred years (and we must do it even better)— maintain a reasonably well-ordered world in which most people can live and work in peace and freedom. The articles of partnership are not yet drawn, but the necessity and desire for them are already in our minds and hearts. Even so, there will be no Utopia after this war. The future will be hard, terribly hard—but not too hard. Mankind can count on John Bull and Uncle Sam. They will do the job.

Faithfully yours,
Lawrence Hunt

I 2